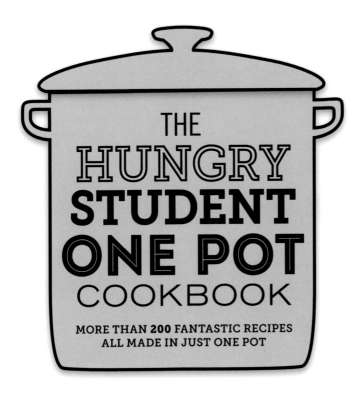

THE HUNGRY STUDENT ONE POT COOKBOOK

**MORE THAN 200 FANTASTIC RECIPES
ALL MADE IN JUST ONE POT**

spruce

An Hachette UK Company
www.hachette.co.uk

First published in Great Britain in 2017 by Spruce,
a division of Octopus Publishing Group Ltd,
Carmelite House, 50 Victoria Embankment,
London EC4Y 0DZ
www.octopusbooks.co.uk

ISBN 978-1-84601-540-3

A CIP catalogue record for this book is available
from the British Library

Printed and bound in China

10 9 8 7 6 5 4 3 2

The recipes in this book have been labelled as
suitable for vegan and vegetarian diets.
Vegetarians should look for the 'V' symbol on
a cheese to ensure it is made with vegetarian
rennet. There are vegetarian forms of Parmesan,
feta, Cheddar, Cheshire, Red Leicester, dolcelatte
and many goats' cheeses, among others.

Standard level spoon measurement are used
in all recipes.
1 tablespoon = one 15 ml spoon
1 teaspoon = one 5 ml spoon

Both imperial and metric measurements have
been given in all recipes. Use one set of
measurements only and not a mixture of both.

Ovens should be preheated to the specific
temperature – if using a fan-assisted oven, follow
manufacturer's instructions for adjusting the
time and the temperature.

Pepper should be freshly ground black pepper
unless otherwise stated.

Recipes that require these special appliances
are indicated with the below icons.

**FOOD
PROCESSOR**

MICROWAVE

**SLOW
COOKER**

Contents

INTRODUCTION

When you move out of home for the first time, hopefully you will have gleaned enough skills to enable you to wash your own clothes, find your way around campus and cook yourself a decent meal. That doesn't mean you need to have perfected the culinary arts but being able to rustle up a passable dinner and expand your repertoire beyond toast and cereal will make mealtimes far more enjoyable.

Cooking everything in one dish is less daunting than having to master a number of different skills and, even if you don't have much experience in the kitchen beyond boiling the kettle or slicing cheese for sandwiches, you should soon be able to create a variety of healthy and tasty meals that will help to keep your limited budget in check.

One-pot cooking minimizes preparation time and washing up, which is good news for anyone who doesn't want to spend hours in the kitchen but still wants to enjoy a home-cooked meal in the evening. It also reduces waste, as many recipes are adaptable – particularly stews and casseroles where you can chuck in any old vegetables and herbs that happen to be lying around, rather than consigning them to the food bin. One-pot cooking also conserves energy because you're not using every ring on the hob, or keeping the oven and hob running at the same time for lengthy periods of time. Plus, a slow cooker uses less energy than a conventional electric oven, even when it has been on for 6 or 7 hours.

KITCHEN EQUIPMENT

Whether you're moving into student accommodation or a shared house, you'll need to bring a certain amount of utensils and equipment with you in order to prepare and cook food. It makes sense to put together a list of what you'll need and divide it up between you and your housemates before moving-in day. That way, you won't end up with a cupboard full of lemon squeezers and garlic crushers but only enough plates and cutlery for two people to eat dinner together.

It's unlikely that you'll be able to afford to splash out on fancy gadgets and designer crockery and there's really no need – between wear and tear, accidents and neglect, the contents of a student kitchen will be put through their paces. However, one-pot cooking means you'll be relying on a large pan, casserole dish and probably another oven-to-table pot – and it's worth spending a little more to buy a couple of pieces of quality cookware that will stay the distance.

ESSENTIAL UTENSILS AND EQUIPMENT

- **Sharp knives** Two good knives should cover all your needs – a large one for meat and fish and a smaller one for paring and cutting vegetables.
- **Utensils** Measuring jug, two mixing bowls, wooden spoon, rolling pin, grater, spatula, chopping board, vegetable peeler, whisk, colander.
- **Handheld blender** You can buy a handheld blender for a few pounds and you'll find this really useful for making soups and sauces.

SLOW COOKER

A number of the recipes in this book are prepared and cooked in a slow cooker. It's worth investing in one as you can use it to cook healthy, hearty meals with the minimum of effort. And if you thought slow cookers were all about casseroles, think again – you can prepare everything from pot-roast chicken to curry and even sponge puddings in them, so they're extremely versatile.

You can buy a good-quality, large-capacity slow cooker for under £30, which is great value, considering the time and money you'll save once you get into the habit of using it regularly. Choose a brand name that you trust and check out online reviews before you decide which one to buy. If you're planning on cooking meals for your housemates, or you want to make extra portions to freeze, then size matters – choose a slow cooker with a capacity of 5–6 litres (5–6 quarts). It's also worth checking that it includes a timer, so it will stop cooking and just keep the food warm if you're away from home.

SLOW COOKER TIPS

- Clean the cooker as soon as possible after use so food doesn't dry solid. Always unplug the slow cooker before cleaning it.
- Don't add extra liquid to the cooker, unless stated in the recipe. The tight-fitting lid stops any liquid from evaporating so the food will stay moist.
- Keep the lid on during cooking – it might be tempting to take a quick peek inside but you'll tamper with the temperature if you do.
- Brown meat in a frying pan before adding it to the slow cooker. Okay, so that's not technically one-pot cooking but it's all in the name of flavour.

STORE-CUPBOARD *staples*

One-pot cookery is perfectly suited to long and slow cooking and you'll need a cupboard full of healthy grains and pulses, as well as a good selection of fresh ingredients, plus herbs and spices to add depth of flavour to your meals.

- **Salt and pepper** Fine salt and ground pepper are ideal for seasoning dishes, while sea salt and freshly ground pepper make a sophisticated addition to the dinner table.
- **Oil** Vegetable oil is a good everyday option for cooking and olive oil is perfect for salad dressings, marinades and sauces.
- **Canned chopped tomatoes** Essential for sauces, soups and stews, this is a cheap and nutritious ingredient that you can buy in bulk.

- **Onions and garlic** These two ingredients are essential in many cuisines and they form the base for a lot of savoury dishes in this book. Make sure you have a steady supply of both onions and garlic in the kitchen.
- **Rice** There are lots of different varieties of rice. You'll need arborio rice if you want to cook risottos and jasmine rice for Thai food. Brown rice is the healthy option but it takes longer to cook so take this into account when you're planning your meals. Pick a couple of the rice varieties that you think you'll use most often and buy in bulk.
- **Pasta** Again, choose just a couple of large packets of the pasta shapes you think you will use most frequently so you don't end up with dozens of different types of pasta filling up your cupboard. Pasta is a student staple and is well suited to one-pot cooking so you'll be eating a lot of it.
- **Cans of beans** Stock up on cheap, protein-rich varieties like kidney beans (great for chillies), borlotti and butter beans (ideal for adding bulk to soups) and chickpeas (perfect for stews, curries and salads.)
- **Lentils** Healthy, nutritious and incredibly cheap, what's not to like about lentils? Red lentils break down when they are cooked for a long time, which makes them really useful for thickening up soups and stews. French Puy lentils hold their shape and are delicious in confits and casseroles.

Meal planning & shopping lists

You'll save a lot of money on your food bill if you plan your meals in advance. By shopping for exactly what you need for each meal, you'll reduce food wastage and avoid costly impulse buys. It only takes a few minutes to work out a rough plan for the week's meals. Cooking together as a household will also save money but it does mean that you'll need to be a bit more organized and get everyone together to agree on the weekly meal plan, cooking rota and food shop.

Don't worry if you can't stick to the plan rigidly – things will crop up during the week, which means people heading out at the last minute, or bringing friends home for dinner. Luckily, one-pot cooking is pretty flexible when it comes to working around a student lifestyle and an extra person at the dinner table shouldn't put a spanner in the works. Likewise, one less for dinner simply means an extra portion that you can store in the fridge or freezer to be eaten another time.

Once you've worked out a rough plan for the week, it makes sense to do one large supermarket shop for all the main ingredients, plus other essentials that you'll need like milk, bread, cereal and fruit. If you don't have a car and don't fancy heaving a week's worth of food for a house full of hungry students on the bus, then online shopping is definitely the most convenient way to buy your groceries. Inevitably, there'll be extras required during the week and a little blackboard or notebook in the kitchen is a handy way to keep track of what's needed. That way, whoever is passing the shops can top up when they go out.

VARIETY IS THE SPICE OF LIFE

When you're planning your meals, take into account any dietary requirements, likes and dislikes so that everyone has a say in the week's menu. Alternatively, if there is a mix of vegetarians and meat-eaters, it might make more sense to prepare different meals. However you organize the cooking and planning, try to include a good variety of meals to keep dinnertime interesting. So, for example:

- **Monday:** casserole – try the Mixed Seafood Casserole (page 145) or Mustardy Squash, Carrot & Sweet Potato Casserole (page 152).
- **Tuesday:** rice dish – try the Bacon, Pea & Courgette Risotto (page 94) or Pork & Tomato Rice Pot (page 131).
- **Wednesday:** veggie meal – try the Veggie Bean Chilli (page 113) or Brown Rice, Mint & Haloumi Pilaf (page 153).
- **Thursday:** Italian night – try the Pizza Fiorentina (page 49) or Spicy Tuna, Tomato & Olive Pasta (page 106).
- **Friday:** fish supper – try the Crispy Fish Pie (page 138) or Oven-baked Fish & Chips with Tomato Salsa (page 144).
- **Saturday:** curry – try the Pea & Lamb Korma (page 137) or Chicken & Caramelized Onion Dhal (page 170).
- **Sunday:** meat lover's Sunday lunch – try the Roast Chicken with Butternut Squash (page 72) or Spicy Pulled Gammon with Apricots (page 177).

HOW TO USE THIS BOOK

Each recipe in the book can be prepared and cooked in just one dish – whether that's a slow cooker, casserole, saucepan, ovenproof dish, or a bowl in the microwave. There is also a number of cold dishes and salads that don't require any cooking at all – all you have to do is mix the ingredients together and serve.

In addition to the one dish, you will also need a few basic kitchen utensils to cook the recipes (see Essential Utensils & Equipment, page 5), and occasionally a recipe will call for a kitchen appliance, such as a microwave, food processor or slow cooker – we've flagged any recipes that need one of these appliances so that they are easy to spot.

Most of the ingredients you need are everyday items that are not costly or difficult to source, though we have included a few more unusual recipes for special occasions and for when you become more confident and creative in the kitchen.

To help you keep within your food budget, each recipe in this book is rated from 1 to 3, with 1s providing end-of-term saviours that can be scraped together for a pittance, and 3s to splash out and impress all your friends.

WHAT'S FOR LUNCH?

PAELLA SOUP

MASALA DHAL & SWEET POTATO

MINTED PEA SOUP

FEEL-GOOD *broth*

2 boneless, skinless chicken
  breasts, about 300 g (10 oz)
  in total
900 ml (1½ pints) cold chicken
  stock (see page 11 for
  homemade)
1 lemon slice
2 teaspoons roughly chopped
  thyme
250 g (8 oz) fresh meat
  cappelletti or small tortellini
salt and pepper
grated Parmesan cheese,
  to serve

Serves **4**
Prep time **5 minutes**
Cooking time **25 minutes**

1 Put the chicken breasts, stock, lemon slice and thyme
in a large saucepan. Bring to a very gentle simmer –
the water should shiver rather than bubble in the pan.
Cover and cook for 15–16 minutes until the chicken is
opaque all the way through. Remove and discard the
lemon slice.

2 Lift the chicken from the liquid with a slotted spoon
and transfer to a plate. When the chicken is cool
enough to handle, shred into large pieces.

3 Bring the stock to a rapid boil and season with salt and
pepper. Add the pasta and cook for 2–3 minutes, adding
the shredded chicken for the last minute of the
cooking time. Serve immediately with a generous
scattering of grated Parmesan.

VARIATION
For a chicken broth with egg, beat 2 eggs well. Follow
the recipe above, removing the soup from the heat
once the pasta is cooked and gradually pouring in the
eggs in a steady stream, stirring as you go. Sprinkle
with 2 tablespoons chopped tarragon and serve.

AFFORDABILITY
1

CHICKEN MULLIGATAWNY

Melt half the butter in a saucepan and fry the chicken thighs in two batches for 5 minutes each, until golden on all sides. Lift out with a slotted spoon on to a plate.

2 Add the remaining butter and fry the onions, carrots and apple, stirring, for 6-8 minutes until lightly browned.

3 Sprinkle in the flour and cook, stirring, for 1 minute. Gradually blend in the stock, then stir in the curry paste, tomato purée and rice. Return the chicken to the pan and bring to a simmer, stirring. Reduce the heat, cover and cook very gently for 1 hour, or until the chicken is cooked through and very tender.

4 Lift the chicken pieces from the soup with a slotted spoon and transfer to a plate. Once cool enough to handle, pull the meat from the bones. Shred half the meat into pieces and return the remainder to the pan. Blend the soup using a handheld blender.

5 Return the shredded chicken to the pan and heat through. Season to taste with salt and pepper. Ladle the soup into serving bowls and serve topped with spoonfuls of yogurt.

COOKING TIP

For a homemade chicken stock, place 1 large chicken carcass or 500 g (1 lb) chicken bones in a large saucepan and add 2 halved, unpeeled onions, 2 roughly chopped carrots, 1 roughly chopped celery stick, several bay leaves and 1 teaspoon black or white peppercorns. Just cover with cold water and bring to a gentle simmer. Reduce the heat to its lowest setting and cook, uncovered, for 2 hours. Strain through a fine sieve and leave to cool. Cover and store in the refrigerator for up to several days or freeze for up to 6 months.

50 g (2 oz) butter
600 g (1 lb 3 oz) bone-in, skinless chicken thighs
2 onions, chopped
2 small carrots, chopped
1 small cooking apple, peeled, cored and chopped
1 tablespoon plain flour
1 litre (1¾ pints) chicken stock (see tip for homemade)
2 tablespoons mild curry paste
2 tablespoons tomato purée
50 g (2 oz) basmati rice
salt and pepper
natural yogurt, to serve

Serves **6**
Prep time **20 minutes**
Cooking time **1½ hours**

Spicy CHICKEN SOUP
WITH AVOCADO

2 tablespoons olive oil
1 onion, chopped
3 garlic cloves, crushed
1 teaspoon chipotle peppers
  in adobo sauce, chopped,
  or Tabasco sauce
2 teaspoons sugar
400 g (13 oz) can chopped
  tomatoes
1 litre (1¾ pints) hot chicken
  stock (see page 11 for
  homemade)
2 ready-cooked chicken
  breasts, torn into strips
1 ripe avocado, peeled, stoned
  and cubed
handful of tortilla chips,
  crushed
4 tablespoons soured cream
handful of chopped fresh
  coriander
salt and pepper

Serves **4**
Prep time **20 minutes**
Cooking time **20 minutes**

1 Heat the oil in a large saucepan. Add the onion and cook
for 5 minutes until softened, then stir in the garlic, chipotle
peppers or Tabasco sauce and sugar. Pour in the tomatoes
and stock, bring to the boil, then reduce the heat and
simmer for 10 minutes.

2 Use a handheld blender to purée the soup until smooth,
then add a little boiling water if it is too thick and season
to taste with salt and pepper.

3 Ladle the soup into serving bowls and scatter the chicken,
avocado and tortilla chips on top. Drizzle with the soured
cream and sprinkle with the chopped coriander.

VARIATION
For a spicy chicken and avocado salad, mix a few drops of
Tabasco sauce with ½ teaspoon ground cumin and 1 tablespoon
olive oil in a bowl. Coat 2 chicken breast fillets, cut into strips, in
the oil. Cook the chicken in a hot griddle pan for 3 minutes on
each side, or until cooked through. In a large bowl, toss together
100 g (3½ oz) mixed salad leaves, 2 chopped tomatoes, 1 sliced
avocado, the chicken, some crushed tortilla chips, the juice of
½ lime and 1 tablespoon olive oil.

AFFORDABILITY **2**

EASY
CHICKEN PHO

750 ml (1¼ pints) chicken stock
(see page 11 for homemade)
1 shallot, chopped
2 garlic cloves, finely chopped
15 g (½ oz) piece of fresh root
ginger, peeled and chopped
¼ teaspoon dried red chilli
flakes
1 tablespoon dark soy sauce
1 teaspoon Thai fish sauce
200 g (7 oz) boneless, skinless
chicken breast, cut into small
pieces
50 g (2 oz) instant rice noodles
75 g (3 oz) bean sprouts

To garnish
2 spring onions, thinly sliced
chopped fresh coriander

Serves **2**
Prep time **10 minutes**
Cooking time **20 minutes**

1 Put the stock, shallot, garlic, ginger, chilli flakes, soy sauce
and fish sauce in a saucepan and bring to a gentle simmer,
making sure the liquid doesn't boil. Cover and cook very
gently for 10 minutes to infuse the flavours.

2 Add the chicken to the pan, stir well and cook gently for
5 minutes. Add the rice noodles and cook for a further
4–5 minutes, stirring frequently, until the noodles are tender.

3 Stir in the bean sprouts and cook for a few seconds until
heated through. Divide between 2 serving bowls and
garnish with the spring onions and chopped coriander.

CHICKEN SWEETCORN
Chowder

1 Place the creamed sweetcorn in a saucepan with the milk and heat, stirring.

2 Add the chicken, sweetcorn kernels and spring onions and season with salt and pepper. Simmer for 5 minutes, stirring occasionally.

3 Blend the cornflour with 1 tablespoon water in a mug, pour into the soup and stir to thicken. Ladle the soup into serving bowls and serve with crusty bread.

VARIATION
For a chicken, bacon and sweetcorn chowder, fry 2 chopped rashers of bacon with 1 chopped onion and 2 chopped potatoes in a knob of butter for 5 minutes. Pour in 500 ml (17 fl oz) milk and simmer for 10 minutes. Stir in 125 g (4 oz) frozen sweetcorn kernels and 175 g (6 oz) chopped ready-cooked chicken. Season to taste with salt and pepper, heat through and serve sprinkled with chopped parsley.

325 g (11 oz) can creamed sweetcorn
450 ml (¾ pint) milk
175 g (6 oz) ready-cooked chicken, torn into pieces
125 g (4 oz) frozen sweetcorn kernels
2 spring onions, chopped
2 teaspoons cornflour
salt and pepper
crusty bread, to serve

Serves **4**
Prep time **5 minutes**
Cooking time **10 minutes**

MASALA DHAL & SWEET POTATO

1 Heat the oil in a saucepan and fry the onions for 5 minutes. Add the garlic, chilli flakes, ginger, garam masala and turmeric and cook, stirring, for 2 minutes.

2 Add the split peas, tomatoes and 750 ml (1¼ pints) of the stock and bring to the boil. Reduce the heat, cover and cook gently for 20 minutes, or until the peas have started to soften, adding more stock if the mixture runs dry.

3 Stir in the sweet potatoes, re-cover and cook for a further 20 minutes, or until the potatoes and peas are tender, adding more stock if necessary to keep the dhal juicy. Tip the spinach into the pan and stir until wilted. Add a little salt to taste. Serve with warm naan breads and mango chutney.

COOKING TIP

For homemade vegetable stock, heat 1 tablespoon vegetable oil in a large saucepan and gently fry 2 unpeeled and roughly chopped onions, 2 each roughly chopped carrots, celery sticks, parsnips and courgettes and 200 g (7 oz) trimmed and sliced mushrooms, stirring frequently, for 10 minutes, or until softened. Add 3 bay leaves and a handful of parsley and thyme sprigs. Pour in 1.5 litres (2½ pints) cold water and bring to the boil. Reduce the heat and simmer very gently, uncovered, for 40 minutes. Strain through a sieve and leave to cool. Cover and store in the refrigerator for up to several days or freeze for up to 6 months.

3 tablespoons vegetable oil
2 onions, chopped
2 garlic cloves, crushed
½ teaspoon dried red chilli flakes
1.5 cm (¾ inch) piece of fresh root ginger, peeled and grated
2 teaspoons garam masala
½ teaspoon ground turmeric
250 g (8 oz) dried split yellow peas, rinsed and drained
200 g (7 oz) can chopped tomatoes
1 litre (1¾ pints) vegetable stock (see tip for homemade)
500 g (1 lb) sweet potatoes, scrubbed and cut into small chunks
200 g (7 oz) spinach, washed and drained
salt

To serve
warm naan breads
mango chutney

Serves **4**
Prep time **15 minutes**
Cooking time **50 minutes**

AFFORDABILITY
1

PESTO LEMON SOUP

1 tablespoon olive oil
1 onion, finely chopped
2 garlic cloves, finely chopped
2 tomatoes, skinned (see tip)
  and chopped
1.2 litres (2 pints) vegetable
  stock (see page 15 for
  homemade)
1 tablespoons shop-bought
  fresh green, plus extra
  to serve
grated zest and juice of 1 lemon
100 g (3½ oz) broccoli, cut into
  small florets and stems sliced
150 g (5 oz) courgettes, diced
100 g (3½ oz) frozen podded
  soya beans
65 g (2½ oz) small dried pasta
  shapes
50 g (2 oz) spinach, washed,
  drained and shredded
salt and pepper
basil leaves, to garnish
  (optional)
olive or sun-dried tomato
  focaccia or ciabatta, to serve

Serves **6**
Prep time **10 minutes**
Cooking time **25 minutes**

1 Heat the oil in a saucepan and gently fry the onion for
5 minutes, or until softened. Add the garlic, tomatoes,
stock, pesto, lemon zest and a little salt and pepper
and simmer gently for 10 minutes.

2 Add the broccoli, courgettes, soya beans and pasta
shapes and simmer for 6 minutes.

3 Stir the spinach and lemon juice into the pan and cook
for 2 minutes, or until the spinach has just wilted and
the pasta is just tender.

4 Ladle the soup into serving bowls, top with extra
spoonfuls of pesto and garnish with a few basil leaves,
if liked. Serve with olive or sun-dried tomato focaccia
or ciabatta.

COOKING TIP

Tomato skins don't soften, even when cooked for
some time, so are worth removing. Pull away the
stalks, make a slit with a knife and place the tomatoes
in a heatproof bowl. Cover with boiling water and
leave to stand for about 30 seconds if the
tomatoes are very ripe, or a couple of
minutes if very firm. Drain and fill the
bowl with cold water. Peel away the
skins and halve or chop the tomatoes
as required.

AFFORDABILITY
1

PAELLA SOUP

1 Heat the oil in a large heavy-based saucepan. Add the onion and chorizo and cook for 2 minutes, or until the onion has softened and the chorizo is lightly browned.

2 Stir in the garlic, then add the tomatoes, stock and saffron, and season to taste with salt and pepper. Bring to the boil, add the chicken and red pepper and simmer for 10-12 minutes or until the chicken is cooked through.

3 Add the rice and peas and cook for 2-3 minutes until heated through. Ladle the soup into serving bowls.

1 tablespoon olive oil
1 onion, finely chopped
250 g (8 oz) chorizo sausage, chopped
2 garlic cloves, crushed
200 g (7 oz) can chopped tomatoes
1 litre (1¾ pints) chicken stock (see page 11 for homemade)
pinch of saffron threads
2 skinless chicken breast fillets, cubed
1 red pepper, cored, deseeded and chopped
250 g (8 oz) ready-cooked rice
50 g (2 oz) frozen peas, defrosted
salt and pepper

Serves **4**
Prep time **15 minutes**
Cooking time **25 minutes**

CHICKPEA & RED PEPPER SOUP

Vegan

2 tablespoons olive oil
1 onion, finely chopped
1 red pepper, cored, deseeded
  and chopped
2 garlic cloves, crushed
2 teaspoons tomato purée
1 teaspoon ground cumin
½ teaspoon ground coriander
pinch of cayenne pepper
pinch of saffron threads
1.5 litres (2½ pints) hot
  vegetable stock (see page
  15 for homemade)
400 g (13 oz) can chickpeas,
  rinsed and drained
125 g (4 oz) couscous
finely grated zest and juice
  of 1 lemon
salt and pepper

To garnish
handful of chopped mint
handful of chopped fresh
  coriander

Serves **4**
Prep time **15 minutes**
Cooking time **20 minutes**

1 Heat the oil in a large heavy-based saucepan. Add the onion and cook for 5 minutes, then add the red pepper, garlic, tomato purée and spices and cook for a further 1 minute.

2 Pour in the stock and bring to the boil, then reduce the heat and simmer for 5 minutes. Add the chickpeas and simmer for a further 5 minutes, then season to taste with salt and pepper.

3 Add the couscous and a squeeze of lemon juice and cook for 1 minute, or until the couscous is tender. Ladle into serving bowls and garnish with the chopped herbs and grated lemon zest.

VARIATION
For a chickpea and red pepper couscous, heat 1 tablespoon olive oil in a large heavy-based saucepan. Add 2 sliced garlic cloves and cook for 1 minute, then add 1 chopped ready-roasted pepper, 200 g (7 oz) canned chickpeas, rinsed and drained, and 200 g (7 oz) couscous. Remove from the heat. Pour in 250 ml (8 fl oz) hot vegetable stock, cover and leave for 5 minutes until tender. Stir in a good squeeze of lemon juice and 75 g (3 oz) rocket.

EAT WELL FOR LESS

It's the age-old student conundrum – how do you eat well on a meagre budget that is already taking the strain of other important commitments like beer, gig nights ... oh, and books. Well luckily, one-pot meals are perfectly suited to upcycling humble everyday fare into incredible dishes that will please your wallet and your taste buds. And, when you do find you have a few spare pennies in your purse, you can splash out on more extravagant ingredients for special occasions.

BUDGET

Before you can start planning what you're going to cook and eat, you need to be aware of exactly how much you have to spend on food. That means looking at your total income and taking off the cost of your rent, bills and other recurring overheads and seeing what's left. You can do this on a monthly or weekly basis and either set aside a specific amount for food, or you can decide each week what you can realistically spend.

Next you need to decide if you're shopping individually, or clubbing together with your housemates. The good thing about buying your food together is that you can take advantage of bulk buys and discounts; the downside is that the kitchen cupboards can end up becoming a bit of a free-for-all, and you won't have exclusive ownership rights to the last slab of cheese or your favourite box of cereal.

SHOP AROUND

Once you've worked out your budget and food sharing arrangements, it's time to work out where you can get the most for your money. If you have more than one supermarket close by, you can try price comparison websites to ensure you're paying the cheapest price for your regular items. Many town centres have fruit and veg stalls and these can offer very good value for money. Plus, if you loiter around the stalls towards the end of the day, you'll find vendors offering massive discounts to clear their stock. Likewise, farmers' markets are worth a trip for good quality seasonal produce. Online shopping can save you time and money – many supermarkets offer free delivery slots at unpopular times (which can work to your advantage as a student).

Don't be tempted by unrealistic offers – will you really work your way through two punnets of peaches in a day?

Pick up bargains at the end of the day and tuck them away in your freezer – this is a great option for meat and fish, which can be expensive.

Don't be afraid to shop around and buy different ingredients from different shops or market stalls.

Nothing beats a Saturday take-out curry or Chinese meal but with a little practice and not much effort you can make your own versions for a fraction of the cost.

Minted PEA SOUP 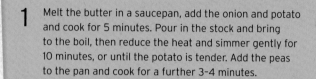 (V)

15 g (½ oz) butter
1 onion, finely chopped
1 potato, finely chopped
1 litre (1¾ pints) vegetable
  stock (see page 15 for
  homemade)
400 g (13 oz) frozen peas
6 tablespoons finely chopped
  mint
salt and pepper
crème fraîche (optional),
  to serve

Serves **4**
Prep time **10 minutes**
Cooking time **20 minutes**

1 Melt the butter in a saucepan, add the onion and potato and cook for 5 minutes. Pour in the stock and bring to the boil, then reduce the heat and simmer gently for 10 minutes, or until the potato is tender. Add the peas to the pan and cook for a further 3–4 minutes.

2 Season well with salt and pepper, then remove from the heat and stir in the mint. Blend the soup using a handheld blender. Ladle into serving bowls and top each portion with a dollop of crème fraîche, if liked.

VARIATION

For a chunky pea and ham soup, cook 1 chopped carrot and 1 chopped turnip with the onion and potato, then add 1 litre (1¾ pints) chicken stock. Once the root vegetables are tender, add 300 g (10 oz) chopped ready-cooked ham, 4 finely chopped spring onions and 2 tablespoons chopped parsley with the peas and cook for 3–4 minutes. Do not blend the soup, but ladle into serving bowls and serve with crusty bread.

AFFORDABILITY **1**

QUINOA &
tomato soup

1 Heat the oil in a saucepan. Add about a third of the kale and fry quickly, stirring continuously, until the kale starts to crisp. Lift out on to a plate with a slotted spoon.

2 Add the onion to the pan and fry for 4–5 minutes until softened. Add the stock and quinoa and bring to a gentle simmer. Cook for about 15 minutes, stirring frequently, until the quinoa is tender.

3 Add the tomatoes, sun-dried tomato paste or tomato purée, sugar, oregano or thyme and paprika and cook for about 10 minutes until the soup has thickened.

4 Stir in the uncooked kale and cook for a further 5 minutes. Season with pepper. Ladle the soup into serving bowls and serve topped with the fried kale.

COOKING TIP
You'll find onions in many of the recipes in this book. If you want to chop them without ending up with red, watery eyes, try one of these tricks: chill them before chopping; chop them in a bowl of cold water; make sure your knife is super sharp for less exposure of cut areas; wear a swim mask when cutting them.

1 tablespoon vegetable or mild olive oil
50 g (2 oz) kale, tough stalks removed, and shredded
1 onion, chopped
500 ml (17 fl oz) vegan stock
50 g (2 oz) quinoa, rinsed
400 g (13 oz) can chopped tomatoes
1 tablespoon sun-dried tomato paste or tomato purée
2 teaspoons brown sugar
1 teaspoon dried oregano or thyme
½ teaspoon paprika
pepper

Serves **2**
Prep time **10 minutes**
Cooking time **35 minutes**

CHORIZO &
BLACK BEAN SOUP

2 tablespoons vegetable oil
1 onion, finely chopped
125 g (4 oz) chorizo sausage,
  finely diced
1 red pepper, cored, deseeded
  and chopped
1 garlic clove, chopped
1 teaspoon ground cumin
1.5 litres (2½ pints) hot chicken
  stock (see page 11 for
  homemade)
2 x 400 g (13 oz) cans black
  beans, rinsed and drained
salt and pepper

To serve
2 tablespoons lime juice
4 tablespoons soured cream
handful of chopped fresh
  coriander
1 red chilli, chopped

Serves **4**
Prep time **15 minutes**
Cooking time **20 minutes**

1 Heat the oil in a large heavy-based saucepan. Add the onion, chorizo, red pepper and garlic and cook for 7–10 minutes until softened, then stir in the cumin. Pour in the stock and beans and simmer for 5–8 minutes.

2 Season to taste with salt and pepper, then use a potato masher to roughly mash some of the beans to thicken the soup. Ladle the soup into serving bowls and sprinkle a little lime juice over each portion. Add a spoonful of soured cream, top with a sprinkling of the chopped coriander and chilli and serve immediately.

VARIATION

For a chorizo and black bean salad, rinse and drain a 400 g (13 oz) can black beans. Put the beans in a bowl and mix with 2 tablespoons extra virgin olive oil and a good squeeze of lime juice. Season to taste with salt and pepper. Add 2 chopped tomatoes, 2 chopped spring onions and a good handful of chopped fresh coriander and toss to combine. Spoon the salad on to a serving plate and arrange slices of fried chorizo sausage on top. Serve with crusty bread.

AFFORDABILITY
1

WINTERY
MINESTRONE
WITH PASTA
& BEANS

1 Heat the oil in a large heavy-based saucepan. Add the onion, celery and carrot and cook for 5 minutes, or until softened, then add the garlic and cook for a further 1 minute.

2 Pour in the tomatoes and stock, add the rosemary and bring to the boil. Reduce the heat and simmer for 15 minutes.

3 Add the pasta and cabbage and cook for 5-7 minutes or according to the packet instructions. Stir in the beans and heat through, then season to taste with salt and pepper. Ladle the soup into serving bowls, drizzle with the pesto, sprinkle with the grated Parmesan and serve with crusty bread.

VARIATION
For a pasta and bean salad, cook 300 g (10 oz) orzo pasta in a large saucepan of lightly salted boiling water for 5 minutes. Drain, cool under cold running water and drain again. Return the drained pasta to the pan. Toss with 200 g (7 oz) canned cannellini beans, rinsed and drained, 150 g (5 oz) halved cherry tomatoes and 125 g (4 oz) rocket. Stir in 4 tablespoons extra virgin olive oil and 1 tablespoon white wine vinegar, season to taste with salt and pepper and serve sprinkled with grated Parmesan.

2 tablespoons olive oil
1 onion, chopped
1 celery stick, chopped
1 carrot, chopped
1 garlic clove, crushed
400 g (13 oz) can chopped tomatoes
1.5 litres (2½ pints) vegetable stock (see page 15 for homemade)
sprig of rosemary
150 g (5 oz) small soup pasta
75 g (3 oz) cavolo nero or other cabbage
200 g (7 oz) canned cannellini beans, rinsed and drained
4 tablespoons shop-bought fresh green pesto
25 g (1 oz) Parmesan cheese, grated
salt and pepper
crusty bread, to serve

Serves **4**
Prep time **15 minutes**
Cooking time **30 minutes**

BALSAMIC ROAST VEG SALAD

Vegan

1 red onion, roughly chopped
4 carrots, roughly chopped
1 red pepper, cored, deseeded
  and cut into large pieces
1 sweet potato, peeled and cut
  into even-sized pieces
400 g (13 oz) courgettes,
  peeled and cut into even-
  sized pieces
1 butternut squash, about 1 kg
  (2 lb), peeled, deseeded and
  cut into chunks
2 tablespoons olive oil, plus
  extra to drizzle
150 ml (¼ pint) balsamic
  vinegar
1 tablespoon chopped thyme
1 tablespoon chopped rosemary
75 g (3 oz) rocket
salt and pepper

Serves **4**
Prep time **20 minutes**
Cooking time **30 minutes**

1 Put all the vegetables in a roasting tin, drizzle over the oil and balsamic vinegar and sprinkle with the herbs. Toss to make sure everything is well coated in the oil, then season to taste. Roast in a preheated oven, 190°C (375°F), Gas Mark 5, for 30 minutes, or until they are cooked and slightly crispy.

2 Remove the vegetables from the oven, allow to cool slightly, then toss with the rocket. Drizzle with olive oil, check the seasoning and serve.

AFFORDABILITY 1

Greek salad
WITH TOASTED PITTA (V)

100 g (3½ oz) feta cheese, crumbled into smallish chunks
8-10 mint leaves, shredded
100 g (3½ oz) kalamata olives, pitted
2 tomatoes, chopped
juice of 1 large lemon
1 small red onion, thinly sliced
1 teaspoon dried oregano
4 pitta breads
lemon wedges, to serve

Serves **4**
Prep time **15 minutes**
Cooking time **5 minutes**

1 Toss together the feta, mint, olives, tomatoes, lemon juice, onion and oregano in a bowl.

2 Toast the pittas under a preheated hot grill until lightly golden, then split open and toast the open sides.

3 Tear the hot pittas into bite-sized pieces, then toss with the other salad ingredients in the bowl. Serve with lemon wedges.

AFFORDABILITY 1

FENNEL, ORANGE & olive salad

 Vegan

1 large fennel bulb, about 325 g (11 oz), thinly sliced
8-10 black olives, pitted
1 tablespoon extra virgin olive oil
2 tablespoons lemon juice
2 oranges
salt and pepper

Serves **4-6**
Prep time **10 minutes**

1 Toss the fennel with the olives, oil and lemon juice in a bowl. Season with salt and pepper.

2 Working over the salad bowl to catch the juice and using a serrated knife, cut away the skin and pith of the oranges and slice thinly into rounds. Add the orange slices to the fennel salad and toss very gently to combine.

AFFORDABILITY
1

CAULI CHEESE
& LEEKS

1 Place the cauliflower and leek in a shallow flameproof casserole and pour in the stock. Cover and simmer for 5 minutes, then pour away half the stock.

2 Blend the cornflour with 3 tablespoons of the remaining stock in a mug, then stir in the crème fraîche. Pour the cornflour mixture into the casserole, add half the Cheddar and cook for 1 minute. Season to taste with salt and pepper.

3 Sprinkle the remaining Cheddar over the vegetables and place in a preheated oven, 200°C (400°F), Gas Mark 6, for 15-20 minutes until golden and bubbling. Serve with crusty bread.

1 cauliflower, cut into florets
1 large leek, trimmed, cleaned and sliced
500 ml (17 fl oz) hot vegetable stock (see page 15 for homemade)
2 tablespoons cornflour
150 ml (¼ pint) crème fraîche
100 g (3½ oz) Cheddar cheese, grated
salt and pepper
crusty bread, to serve

Serves **4**
Prep time **10 minutes**
Cooking time **30 minutes**

Eat-&-run SPINACH & CHICKPEA PITTAS

1 Heat the oil in a frying pan, add the onion and fry, stirring, for 3-4 minutes until softened. Add the curry paste, tomato purée, honey and the measured water and stir to mix. Add the chickpeas and cook for 5 minutes, or until hot and bubbling. Most of the water should have evaporated and the juices thickened.

2 Lightly toast the pitta breads while you stir the spinach into the chickpeas until just wilted. Season to taste with salt and pepper.

3 Split the pitta breads and spoon in the filling. Top with a little yogurt and serve.

1 tablespoon vegetable oil
1 small onion, sliced
1 teaspoon medium curry paste
1 tablespoon tomato purée
1 teaspoon clear honey
100 ml (3½ fl oz) water
200 g (7 oz) canned chickpeas, rinsed and drained
2 pitta breads
75 g (3 oz) baby spinach leaves
2 tablespoons Greek yogurt
salt and pepper

Serves **2**
Prep time **10 minutes**
Cooking time **10 minutes**

MELTED CHEESE
& chicken
TORTILLA WEDGES

AFFORDABILITY
2

1 Lay 4 tortillas on 2 large baking sheets and scatter with the chicken, red peppers and chilli. Divide the chorizo and cheeses between the tortillas and sprinkle over the coriander. Season to taste with salt and pepper.

2 Place another tortilla on top of each to make a sandwich, then gently press down with your hand. Place in a preheated oven, 190°C (375°F), Gas Mark 5, and cook for 7 minutes, or until lightly crisp and the cheese has melted. Cut into wedges and serve with guacamole.

8 corn or wheat tortillas
2 ready-cooked chicken breasts, torn into shreds
2 ready-roasted red peppers, torn into strips
1 red chilli, finely chopped
100 g (3½ oz) chorizo sausage, thinly sliced
200 g (7 oz) mozzarella cheese, thinly sliced
50 g (2 oz) mature Cheddar cheese, grated
handful of chopped fresh coriander
salt and pepper
ready-made guacamole, to serve

Serves **4**
Prep time **15 minutes**
Cooking time **10 minutes**

CHICKEN, OLIVE & CUMIN
COUSCOUS

1 Heat the oil in a saucepan, add the lemon and cook over a gentle heat for about 2 minutes until the lemon is soft. Stir in the honey, cumin and garlic and heat through. Stir in the couscous, stock, chickpeas, olives and chicken.

2 Remove from the heat and leave to stand for 5 minutes, or until the couscous is tender. Fluff up the couscous with a fork and stir in the coriander and mint. Season to taste with salt and pepper and serve immediately.

VARIATION
For cumin-dusted chicken breasts with spicy olive couscous, heat 2 tablespoons oil in a frying pan. Dust 4 small chicken breast fillets with 1 teaspoon ground cumin, season with salt and pepper and cook for 5 minutes on each side, or until just cooked through. Stir in 1 crushed garlic clove and 2 teaspoons harissa or chilli paste. Add 250 g (8 oz) couscous, 300 ml (½ pint) hot chicken stock and 50 g (2 oz) green olives, pitted. Cover and leave to stand for 5 minutes, or until the couscous is tender. Fluff up the couscous with a fork and stir in a handful each of chopped mint and fresh coriander and the grated zest and juice of ½ lemon.

4 tablespoons olive oil
rind and flesh of ½ lemon, finely chopped
1 tablespoon clear honey
½ teaspoon ground cumin
1 garlic clove, crushed
300 g (10 oz) couscous
300 ml (½ pint) hot chicken stock (see page 11 for homemade)
400 g (13 oz) can chickpeas, rinsed and drained
50 g (2 oz) green olives, pitted
2 ready-cooked chicken breasts, sliced
handful each of chopped fresh coriander and mint
salt and pepper

Serves **4**
Prep time **10 minutes, plus standing**
Cooking time **5 minutes**

CHICKEN, LENTILS & KALE

1   Heat half the oil in a large frying pan with a lid. Add the chicken, season to taste with salt and pepper and cook for 5 minutes, then turn over and cook for a further 2 minutes, or until golden all over.

2   Add the remaining oil to the pan along with the garlic, kale and a splash of water. Cover and cook for 7 minutes, or until the kale is tender and the chicken cooked through.

3   Stir in the lentils and heat through, then add the lemon juice and tomatoes. Taste and adjust the seasoning if necessary.

4   Lift the chicken breasts from the pan with a slotted spoon and transfer to a plate. Cut the chicken into thick slices and arrange on serving plates with the lentils and kale. Scatter over the goats' cheese and serve immediately.

2 tablespoons olive oil
4 skinless chicken breast fillets
1 garlic clove, sliced
100 g (3½ oz) kale, tough stalks removed, and chopped
250 g (8 oz) can Puy lentils, rinsed and drained
2 tablespoons lemon juice
75 g (3 oz) sun-blush tomatoes
75 g (3 oz) soft goats' cheese, crumbled
salt and pepper

Serves **4**
Prep time **10 minutes**
Cooking time **15 minutes**

AFFORDABILITY 2

CHICKEN
pad Thai

3 tablespoons vegetable oil
1 egg, lightly beaten
1 garlic clove, crushed
2 teaspoons finely grated fresh
   root ginger
2 spring onions, sliced
300 g (10 oz) ready-cooked rice
   noodles
50 g (2 oz) bean sprouts
2 ready-cooked chicken
   breasts, torn into thin strips
2 tablespoons Thai fish sauce
2 teaspoons tamarind paste
2 teaspoons caster sugar
pinch of chilli powder

To garnish
25 g (1 oz) ready-roasted
   peanuts, roughly chopped
handful of chopped fresh
   coriander

Serves **4**
Prep time **10 minutes**
Cooking time **10 minutes**

1 Heat a large wok until smoking hot. Add 1 tablespoon of the oil and swirl around the pan, then pour in the egg. Stir around the pan and cook for 1–2 minutes until just cooked through. Lift the egg from the wok with a slotted spoon and transfer to a plate.

2 Heat the remaining oil in the wok, add the garlic, ginger and spring onions and cook for 2 minutes, or until softened. Add the noodles, bean sprouts and chicken to the wok. Stir in the fish sauce, tamarind paste, sugar and chilli powder and continue to cook, adding a splash of boiling water if necessary, until heated through.

3 Return the egg to the pan and mix in. Divide among serving bowls and garnish with the chopped peanuts and coriander.

VARIATION
For a chicken noodle soup, put 1.2 litres (2 pints) chicken stock in a saucepan with 3 tablespoons rice wine, 2 tablespoons light soy sauce and 1 star anise and simmer for 10 minutes. Mix 300 g (10 oz) minced chicken with 1 teaspoon grated fresh root ginger and 1 teaspoon soy sauce in a bowl. Shape the chicken mixture into balls and cook in the soup for 7 minutes. Add 100 g (3½ oz) shiitake mushrooms and cook for a further 3 minutes. Stir in 2 bok choi, quartered, and cook for 1 minute. Add 200 g (7 oz) ready-cooked rice noodles and cook until heated through.

RÖSTI *with* SMOKED SALMON & ROCKET SALAD

1 Place the potatoes and onion in a clean tea towel and squeeze to remove excess moisture. Season well with salt and pepper.

2 Heat the butter and 1 tablespoon of the oil in a nonstick frying pan. Tip in the potato mixture and spread out to make an even layer, then cook for about 10 minutes, or until the underside is golden. Invert the rösti on to a plate, then carefully slide it back into the pan to cook the other side. Cook for a further 5–8 minutes until cooked through and golden all over.

3 Meanwhile, make the rocket salad. Mix the lemon juice with the remaining oil in a bowl and toss with the rocket.

4 Cut the rösti into wedges and serve with the rocket salad, slices of smoked salmon and lemon wedges.

VARIATION

For a smoked salmon and rocket pasta, cook 500 g (1 lb) fresh penne in a large saucepan of lightly salted boiling water according to the packet instructions. Drain and return to the pan. Add 4 tablespoons crème fraîche, 2 tablespoons lemon juice and 175 g (6 oz) smoked salmon, cut into strips. Toss through 75 g (3 oz) rocket and season to taste with salt and pepper just before serving.

750 g (1½ lb) waxy potatoes, coarsely grated
1 small onion, coarsely grated
50 g (2 oz) butter
3 tablespoons olive oil
2 tablespoons lemon juice
100 g (3½ oz) rocket
salt and pepper

To serve
250 g (8 oz) smoked salmon
lemon wedges

Serves **4**
Prep time **10 minutes**
Cooking time **20 minutes**

Zingy PRAWN WRAPS

AFFORDABILITY
2

1 Prepare the rice wrappers according to the packet instructions.

2 Toss together all the remaining ingredients in a bowl. Divide the mixture evenly among the wrappers and roll up, ensuring the ends are tucked in. Serve straight away.

12 rice wrappers
150 g (5 oz) ready-cooked peeled prawns, shredded
1 carrot, peeled and cut into very fine matchsticks
¼ cucumber, cut into very fine matchsticks
1 small bunch of fresh coriander, chopped
8 mint leaves, chopped
½ mango, peeled and cut into small strips
1 teaspoon sesame oil
1 teaspoon lime juice
handful of peanuts, roughly chopped (optional)
½ red chilli, deseeded and finely chopped (optional)

Makes **12**
Prep time **15 minutes**

STUDENT TIP

Even if you lack outdoor space you can still grow your own salad leaves and herbs — a few pots on the windowsill is all you need for a collection of fresh ingredients that will liven up pasta sauces, casseroles and salads for the price of a few packets of seeds.

Caramelized PARSNIPS

625 g (1¼ lb) parsnips,
  scrubbed or peeled
50 g (2 oz) butter
175 g (6 oz) diced bacon
3 tablespoons caster sugar
50 g (2 oz) pine nuts
5 tablespoons chopped thyme

Serves **2**
Prep time **5 minutes**
Cooking time **20 minutes**

1 Cut the parsnips in half widthways, then cut the chunky tops into quarters lengthways and the slim bottom halves in half lengthways.

2 Heat the butter in a large frying pan, add the bacon and parsnips and cook over a medium heat for about 15 minutes, turning and tossing occasionally, until the parsnips are golden and softened and the bacon is crisp.

3 Add the sugar and pine nuts and cook for a further 2–3 minutes until lightly caramelized. Toss with the thyme and serve.

VARIATION
For a bacon, pine nut and parsnip rösti, grate 350 g (11½ oz) peeled parsnips into a bowl and mix with 50 g (2 oz) ready-cooked bacon rashers, snipped into small pieces, and 2 tablespoons chopped parsley. Divide the mixture and squeeze together to form 4 balls, then flatten into patties. Heat 50 g (2 oz) butter in a large frying pan, add the patties and cook over a high heat for 2 minutes on each side, or until golden. Serve hot with a green salad and sprinkled with pine nuts.

AFFORDABILITY 1

SPICY MUSHROOMS & CAULI ⓥ

2 tablespoons sunflower oil
8 spring onions, cut into 5 cm
 (2 inch) lengths
2 teaspoons grated garlic
2 teaspoons ground ginger
2 tablespoons hot curry
 powder
200 g (7 oz) baby button
 mushrooms
300 g (10 oz) cauliflower florets
2 red peppers, cored, deseeded
 and cut into chunks
400 g (13 oz) can chopped
 tomatoes
200 g (7oz) canned chickpeas,
 rinsed and drained
salt and pepper
large handful of chopped mint,
 to garnish
warm naan breads, to serve

Serves **4**
Prep time **10 minutes**
Cooking time **25 minutes**

1 Heat the oil in a large frying pan, add the spring onions and fry over a medium heat for 1-2 minutes. Add the garlic, ginger and curry powder and fry, stirring, for 20-30 seconds until fragrant, then stir in the mushrooms, cauliflower and red peppers and fry for a further 2-3 minutes.

2 Stir in the tomatoes and bring to the boil. Reduce the heat to medium and simmer for 10-15 minutes, stirring occasionally. Add the chickpeas, season with salt and pepper and bring back to the boil. Garnish with the chopped mint and serve with warm naan breads.

VARIATION

For a spicy mushroom, cauliflower and chickpea rice, heat 2 tablespoons sunflower oil in a large frying pan until hot, add 1 chopped onion, 1 deseeded and chopped red chilli, 100 g (3½ oz) baby button mushrooms, 1 tablespoon curry powder, 100 g (3½ oz) small cauliflower florets, 100 g (3½ oz) canned chickpeas, rinsed and drained, 1 teaspoon ginger paste and 1 teaspoon garlic paste and stir-fry over a high heat for 6-8 minutes. Add 500 g (1 lb) ready-cooked basmati or long-grain rice and stir-fry for a further 3-4 minutes until piping hot. Season with salt and pepper, then serve immediately.

AFFORDABILITY 1

flash-in-the-pan RATATOUILLE

Vegan

100 ml (3½ fl oz) olive oil
2 onions, chopped
1 aubergine, cut into 1.5 cm
    (¾ inch) cubes
2 large courgettes, cut into
    1.5 cm (¾ inch) cubes
1 red pepper, cored, deseeded
    and cut into 1.5 cm (¾ inch)
    pieces
1 yellow pepper, cored,
    deseeded and cut into 1.5 cm
    (¾ inch) pieces
2 garlic cloves, crushed
400 g (13 oz) can chopped
    tomatoes
2-3 tablespoons balsamic
    vinegar
1 teaspoon soft brown sugar
salt and pepper

To garnish
10-12 black olives, pitted
torn basil leaves

Serves **4**
Prep time **15 minutes**
Cooking time **20 minutes**

AFFORDABILITY
1

1 Heat the oil in a large saucepan until very hot. Add all of the vegetables, except the tomatoes, and stir-fry for a few minutes.

2 Add the tomatoes, balsamic vinegar and sugar, season with salt and pepper and stir well. Cover tightly and simmer for 15 minutes, or until the vegetables are cooked.

3 Remove from the heat, scatter over the olives and torn basil leaves and serve.

VARIATION
For a Mediterranean-style thick vegetable soup, follow the recipe above, then add 300 ml (½ pint) hot vegetable stock to the cooked ratatouille and use a handheld blender to blend until fairly smooth. Ladle the soup into serving bowls and garnish with basil leaves.

TREACLE & MUSTARD BEANS

1 Put all the ingredients in a flameproof casserole and bring slowly to the boil, stirring occasionally.

2 Cover, transfer to a preheated oven, 160°C (325°F), Gas Mark 3, and bake for 1 hour. Remove the lid and bake for a further 30 minutes. Serve with garlic-rubbed bread.

ACCOMPANIMENT TIP
For a garlic-rubbed bread, to serve as an accompaniment, heat a griddle pan until hot, add 6 thick slices of sourdough bread and cook for 2 minutes on each side until lightly charred. Rub each bread slice with a peeled garlic clove (or 2) and drizzle with extra virgin olive oil.

1 carrot, diced
1 celery stick, chopped
1 onion, chopped
2 garlic cloves, crushed
2 x 400 g (13 oz) cans soya beans, drained
700 g (1 lb 7 oz) passata
75 g (3 oz) smoked bacon rashers, diced
2 tablespoons black treacle
2 teaspoons Dijon mustard
salt and pepper
Garlic-rubbed Bread (see tip), to serve

Serves **6**
Prep time **10 minutes**
Cooking time **1 hour 35 minutes**

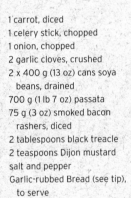

Spiced SWEETCORN
WITH AVOCADO & TOMATO

2 sweetcorn cobs
3 tablespoons sunflower oil
1 red pepper, halved
  lengthways, cored and
  deseeded
1 ripe avocado
½ Scotch bonnet chilli or hot
  red chilli, deseeded and finely
  chopped
6 plum tomatoes, roughly
  chopped
1 small bunch of fresh
  coriander, leaves roughly
  chopped
juice of 2 limes
150 ml (¼ pint) extra virgin
  olive oil
salt and pepper
warm flatbreads, to serve

Serves **4**
Prep time **20 minutes, plus
  cooling**
Cooking time **20 minutes**

1 Blanch the sweetcorn cobs in a large saucepan of boiling water for 30–45 seconds. Drain, then brush the cobs with sunflower oil and cook under a grill preheated to its highest setting for 4–5 minutes, turning frequently, until beginning to char at the edges. Using a sharp knife, cut the kernels from the cobs and put in a large bowl.

2 Cook the red pepper halves, skin-side up, under the preheated grill for 6–8 minutes until the skin begins to blister. Place in a plastic food bag, seal and leave for 5 minutes. When cool, peel away the blackened skin, then dice the flesh and add to the bowl of sweetcorn.

3 Halve, peel and stone the avocado, then dice the flesh. Stir into the sweetcorn mixture with the chilli and tomatoes.

4 Make the dressing. Mix together the coriander, lime juice and olive oil in a mug, then season with salt and pepper and whisk well.

5 Pour the dressing over the sweetcorn mixture and toss through gently. Serve with warm flatbreads.

Stir-fried veg RICE

 Vegan

2 tablespoons sunflower oil
6 spring onions, cut diagonally into 2.5 cm (1 inch) lengths
2 garlic cloves, crushed
1 teaspoon finely grated fresh root ginger
1 red pepper, cored, deseeded and finely chopped
1 carrot, peeled and finely diced
300 g (10 oz) peas
500 g (1 lb) ready-cooked long-grain rice
1 tablespoon dark soy sauce
1 tablespoon sweet chilli sauce
chopped fresh coriander and mint, to garnish

Serves **4**
Prep time **10 minutes**
Cooking time **15 minutes**

1 Heat the oil in a large nonstick wok. Add the spring onions, garlic and ginger and stir-fry over a high heat for 4-5 minutes, then add the red pepper, carrot and peas and stir-fry for 3-4 minutes.

2 Stir in the rice and soy and sweet chilli sauces and stir-fry for 3-4 minutes until the rice is heated through and piping hot. Remove from the heat and serve immediately, garnished with the chopped herbs.

SPINACH & POTATO TORTILLA Ⓥ

3 tablespoons olive oil
2 onions, finely chopped
250 g (8 oz) ready-cooked potatoes, peeled and cut into 1 cm (½ inch) cubes
2 garlic cloves, finely chopped
200 g (7 oz) ready-cooked spinach, drained thoroughly and roughly chopped
4 tablespoons finely chopped ready-roasted red pepper
5 eggs, lightly beaten
3-4 tablespoons grated Manchego cheese
salt and pepper

Serves **4**
Prep time **15 minutes**
Cooking time **20 minutes**

1 Heat the oil in an ovenproof, nonstick frying pan. Add the onions and potatoes and cook gently over a medium heat for 3-4 minutes, turning and stirring often, until the vegetables have softened but not coloured. Stir in the garlic, spinach and red pepper.

2 Season the eggs with salt and pepper, then pour them into the frying pan, shaking the pan so that the egg is evenly spread. Cook gently for 8-10 minutes until the tortilla is set at the bottom.

3 Sprinkle over the cheese. Place the frying pan under a preheated medium-hot grill and cook for 3-4 minutes until the top is set and golden.

4 Cut the tortilla into bite-sized squares or triangles and serve warm or at room temperature.

VARIATION
For a spinach and potato sauté, heat 1 tablespoon vegetable oil in a large frying pan. Add 2 chopped garlic cloves, 1 finely chopped onion and 1 tablespoon curry powder. Stir in 100 ml (3½ fl oz) passata, 300 g (10 oz) baby spinach leaves and 200 g (7 oz) ready-cooked potatoes, cubed. Sauté over a high heat for 2-3 minutes until piping hot. Season with salt and pepper and serve with crusty bread or boiled rice.

TORTILLA
with tomato & rocket salad

1. Heat the olive oil in an ovenproof nonstick frying pan. Add the onion and potato and cook for 5-10 minutes until golden, then pour in the measured water. Simmer gently until the potatoes are very tender, then carefully pour away any excess liquid.

2. Season the eggs with salt and pepper, then pour them into the pan and stir gently. Cook over a low heat for 10-15 minutes until set all the way through, finishing off under a preheated grill to set the top if necessary.

3. To make the salad, toss the rocket with the extra virgin olive oil, lemon juice and tomatoes in a bowl. Season well with salt and pepper and add the Parmesan shavings.

4. To serve, cut the tortilla into wedges and serve topped with the salad.

VARIATION
For egg, tomato and rocket wraps, crack 4 eggs into a lightly greased nonstick frying pan. Dot with 50 g (2 oz) mascarpone cheese and season well with salt and pepper. Cook over a low heat for 2-3 minutes until starting to set. Stir in 1 chopped tomato and cook for a further 1 minute, or until just set. Spoon over 4 wheat tortilla wraps, then scatter with 50 g (2 oz) rocket and a little crumbled goats' cheese. Wrap up the tortillas and serve.

4 tablespoons olive oil
1 onion, finely chopped
3 potatoes, thickly sliced
200 ml (7 fl oz) water
5 eggs, beaten

Tomato & rocket salad
75 g (3 oz) rocket
2 tablespoons extra virgin olive oil
2 tablespoons lemon juice
50 g (2 oz) sun-blush tomatoes
handful of Parmesan cheese shavings
salt and pepper

Serves **4**
Prep time **10 minutes**
Cooking time **20-30 minutes**

AFFORDABILITY
1

PAN-COOKED *eggs* (V)

25 g (1 oz) butter
1 leek, trimmed, cleaned and thinly sliced
½ teaspoon dried red chilli flakes
300 g (10 oz) baby spinach leaves
2 eggs
3 tablespoons natural yogurt
pinch of paprika
salt and pepper

Serves **2**
Prep time **5 minutes**
Cooking time **10 minutes**

1 Heat the butter in a frying pan, add the leek and chilli flakes and cook over a medium-high heat for 4-5 minutes until softened. Add the spinach and season well with salt and pepper, then toss and cook for 2 minutes until the spinach has wilted.

2 Make 2 hollows in the vegetables and break an egg into each hollow. Cook over a low heat for 2-3 minutes until the eggs are set. Spoon the yogurt on top and sprinkle with the paprika.

STUDENT TIP

Don't rely on corner shops and convenience stores for your groceries. Plan in advance and shop at larger supermarkets and food markets — your shopping will be much cheaper.

PIZZA FIORENTINA

125 g (4 oz) baby spinach
   leaves
4 large wheat tortillas
   or flatbreads
150 ml (¼ pint) ready-made
   tomato sauce
125 g (4 oz) mozzarella cheese,
   sliced
4 eggs
25 g (1 oz) Parmesan cheese,
   grated

Serves **4**
Prep time **10 minutes**
Cooking time **10 minutes**

1   Place the spinach in a sieve and pour over boiling water from the kettle until it has wilted, then squeeze thoroughly to remove excess water.

2   Arrange the tortillas on 4 pizza trays. Spoon the tomato sauce over the tortillas, then scatter over the spinach and arrange the mozzarella on top. Crack an egg in the centre of each pizza.

3   Sprinkle the Parmesan over the pizzas, then place in a preheated oven, 220°C (425°F), Gas Mark 7, for 5–7 minutes until the egg whites are just set.

AFFORDABILITY
1

PECORINO & CHILLI
Omelette Ⓥ

1 tablespoon butter
1 egg, lightly beaten
25 g (1 oz) pecorino cheese, grated
pinch of dried red chilli flakes
green salad, to serve

Serves **1**
Prep time **5 minutes**
Cooking time **10 minutes**

1 Heat the butter in a small frying pan until foaming. Pour in the egg and stir around the pan, then leave to cook for 30 seconds until starting to set. Sprinkle over the pecorino and chilli flakes and cook until the omelette is set. Roll up the omelette and serve with a green salad.

STUDENT TIP

Local farmers' markets overflow with great-value seasonal produce and this is the time to really put your freezer to work: wash and bag up seasonal berries; peel and chop apples and pears; and peel and dice vegetables — ready to prepare casseroles, compotes and soups.

AFFORDABILITY
1

Cheesy TURKEY & CRANBERRY MELTS

1   Split the rolls in half and spread the base of each one with the mustard and the top halves of each one with the cranberry sauce. Arrange the turkey slices and cheese on top of the mustard and sandwich the rolls together.

2   Heat a dry frying pan until hot, add the sandwiches and cook over a medium-high heat for 4 minutes on each side, or until golden and the cheese has melted. Serve hot.

VARIATION

For avocado, blue cheese and spinach melts, split the rolls in half and spread the base of each one with a little butter. Mash together 1 peeled, stoned and sliced avocado, 50 g (2 oz) crumbled blue cheese and 2 tablespoons thick cream in a bowl. Divide the avocado mixture between the roll bases, add a few baby spinach leaves and then add the roll tops. Cook as above until the filling starts to ooze.

4 flat rolls
2 tablespoons wholegrain mustard
2 tablespoons cranberry sauce
200 g (7 oz) ready-cooked turkey breast, sliced
125 g (4 oz) Cheddar cheese, grated

Serves **4**
Prep time **5 minutes**
Cooking time **10 minutes**

Egg pots
WITH SMOKED SALMON

butter, for greasing
200 g (7 oz) smoked salmon
  trimmings
2 tablespoons chopped chives
4 eggs
4 tablespoons double cream
toasted bread, to serve
pepper

Serves **4**
Prep time **5 minutes**
Cooking time **10-15 minutes**

1 Grease 4 ramekins with butter. Divide the smoked salmon and chives among the prepared ramekins. Using the back of a spoon, make a small hollow in the top of the salmon in each ramekin. Break an egg into each hollow, sprinkle with a little pepper and spoon the cream over the top.

2 Put the ramekins in a roasting tin and half-fill the tin with boiling water. Bake in a preheated oven, 180°C (350°F), Gas Mark 4, for 10-15 minutes until the eggs have just set.

3 Remove from the oven and leave to cool for a few minutes, then serve with the toasted bread.

ACCOMPANIMENT TIP
For a homemade Melba toast, to serve as an accompaniment, toast 4 slices of bread lightly on both sides. While hot, trim off the crusts, then split the toast in half widthways. Lay the toast, cut-side up, on a baking sheet and bake in the bottom of the oven until dry.

AFFORDABILITY
2

COURGETTE & RICOTTA BAKES

1. Lightly grease 8 holes in a large muffin tin with butter. Use a vegetable peeler to make 16 long ribbons of courgette and set aside. Coarsely grate the remainder of the courgettes on to a clean tea towel and squeeze to remove excess moisture.

2. To make the filling, mix the grated courgette with the remaining ingredients in a bowl and season well with salt and pepper.

3. Arrange 2 courgette ribbons in a cross shape in each hole of the prepared muffin tin. Spoon in the filling and fold over the overhanging courgette ends. Place in a preheated oven, 190°C (375°F), Gas Mark 5, for 15-20 minutes until golden and cooked through. Turn out on to serving plates.

VARIATION
For penne with courgettes and ricotta, cook 500 g (1 lb) fresh penne pasta in a large saucepan of lightly salted boiling water according to the packet instructions, adding 75 g (3 oz) frozen peas for the last 2 minutes of cooking time. Drain and return the pasta and peas to the pan. Add the finely grated zest of 1 lemon and 2 tablespoons lemon juice. Use a vegetable peeler to slice 2 courgettes into long ribbons. Add the courgette ribbons to the pan with 50 g (2 oz) rocket, 2 tablespoons olive oil and 25 g (1 oz) grated Parmesan cheese. Season to taste with salt and pepper. Divide among serving bowls and top with a spoonful of ricotta cheese.

butter, for greasing
2 courgettes
100 g (3½oz) fresh white breadcrumbs
250 g (8 oz) ricotta cheese
75 g (3 oz) Parmesan cheese, grated
2 eggs, beaten
1 garlic clove, crushed
handful of chopped basil
salt and pepper

Serves **4**
Prep time **10 minutes**
Cooking time **15-20 minutes**

AFFORDABILITY
1

Stuffed COURGETTES

1 Slice the courgettes in half horizontally and then scoop out the middle of each one, reserving the flesh. Place the courgette halves, cut-side up, in a roasting tin and bake in a preheated oven, 200°C (400°F), Gas Mark 6, for 10 minutes.

2 Meanwhile, to make the filling, chop the reserved courgette flesh and mix it in a bowl with the tomatoes, mozzarella and basil. Season to taste with salt and pepper.

3 Remove the courgette halves from the oven and spoon the filling into each one. Sprinkle with the Parmesan and return to the oven for 15 minutes, or until golden.

VARIATION
For griddled courgettes with mozzarella, use a vegetable peeler to thinly slice 4 courgettes lengthways. Toss the courgettes in a bowl with 2 tablespoons olive oil and then cook them on a preheated hot griddle pan for 2-3 minutes on both sides, until griddle marks start to show. Served topped with 200 g (7 oz) torn mozzarella cheese and 6-8 torn basil leaves. Drizzle with a little olive oil, a squeeze of lemon juice and a grinding of pepper.

4 courgettes
175 g (6 oz) plum tomatoes, chopped
200 g (7 oz) mozzarella cheese, grated
2 tablespoons shredded basil
25 g (1 oz) Parmesan cheese, grated
salt and pepper

Serves **4**
Prep time **10 minutes**
Cooking time **25 minutes**

feta-stuffed
PEPPERS

1 tablespoon olive oil
4 long peppers
2 egg yolks
200 g (7 oz) feta cheese, crumbled
3 tablespoons natural yogurt
finely grated zest of ½ lemon
1 teaspoon chopped oregano

....

Serves **4**
Prep time **10 minutes, plus cooling**
Cooking time **10-15 minutes**

....

1 Rub the oil over the long peppers, arrange them in a grill pan and cook under a preheated hot grill for 5 minutes, turning once, until just soft. Leave to cool for a couple of minutes, then cut in half lengthways and remove the seeds.

2 Place the egg yolks, three-quarters of the feta, the yogurt and lemon zest in a food processor and blend until smooth. (If you don't have a food processor, put the ingredients in a bowl, mash the feta with a fork and then beat until smooth.) Spoon the mixture into the peppers, then crumble the remaining feta on top and sprinkle with the oregano.

3 Return to the grill and cook for 5-7 minutes until golden and cooked through. Leave to set for a couple of minutes before serving.

VARIATION
For a feta and pepper salad, mash 100 g (3½ oz) feta cheese with 2 tablespoons double cream in a bowl until well combined and smooth. Spoon the mixture over 4 ready-roasted pepper halves and roll up. Make a dressing by whisking 1 tablespoon lemon juice with 3 tablespoons olive oil and ½ teaspoon dried oregano in a separate bowl, then season to taste with salt and pepper. Toss the dressing together with 100 g (3½ oz) lambs' lettuce, ½ sliced cucumber and 50 g (2 oz) pitted black olives. Arrange the salad on a serving platter, cut the peppers into thick slices and arrange on top. Serve with crusty bread.

AFFORDABILITY

VEGETABLE BOLOGNESE

1 Heat the oil in a large heavy-based saucepan. Add the onion, garlic, celery, carrot and mushrooms and cook over a medium heat, stirring frequently, for 5 minutes, or until softened. Add the tomato purée and cook, stirring, for a further 1 minute.

2 Pour in the tomatoes and wine or stock, then add the dried herbs, yeast extract and vegetable protein. Bring to the boil, then reduce the heat, cover and simmer for 30-40 minutes until the vegetable protein is tender.

3 Stir in the parsley and season well with salt and pepper. Divide the sauce between serving plates and serve immediately with cooked spaghetti and a scattering of grated Parmesan.

1 tablespoon vegetable oil
1 onion, finely chopped
1 garlic clove, finely chopped
1 celery stick, finely chopped
1 carrot, finely chopped
75 g (3 oz) chestnut mushrooms, roughly chopped
1 tablespoon tomato purée
400 g (13 oz) can chopped tomatoes
250 ml (8 fl oz) red wine or vegetable stock (see page 15 for homemade)
pinch of dried mixed herbs
1 teaspoon yeast extract
150 g (5 oz) textured vegetable protein (TVP)
2 tablespoons chopped parsley
salt and pepper

To serve
cooked spaghetti
grated Parmesan cheese

Serves **2**
Prep time **10 minutes**
Cooking time **40-50 minutes**

Baked MUSHROOMS
WITH GOATS' CHEESE & ROCKET

500 g (1 lb) new potatoes,
  halved
3 tablespoons olive oil
200 g (7 oz) portobello
  mushrooms
2 tablespoons chopped thyme
6 garlic cloves, unpeeled
50 g (2 oz) soft goats' cheese
125 g (4 oz) cherry tomatoes
salt and pepper
25 g (1 oz) toasted pine nuts,
  to garnish
75 g (3 oz) rocket, to serve

Serves **4**
Prep time **5 minutes**
Cooking time **25 minutes**

1 Put the potatoes in a large roasting tin, drizzle over 2 tablespoons olive oil and toss to make sure the potatoes are well coated in oil. Bake in a preheated oven, 220°C (425°F), Gas Mark 7, for 15 minutes, turning once halfway through the cooking time.

2 Add the mushrooms, stem-side up, to the tin, scatter over the thyme an garlic, drizzle over the remaining oil and season well with salt and pepper. Place a little goats' cheese on top of each mushroom and return to the oven for a further 5 minutes.

3 Add the cherry tomatoes to the tin and return to the oven for 5 minutes more, or until the potatoes and mushrooms are cooked through. Garnish with the pine nuts and serve with the rocket.

VARIATION

For mushroom burgers with goats' cheese and rocket, place 4 large portobello mushrooms on a lightly greased baking sheet and season well. Bake in a preheated oven, 220°C (425°F), Gas Mark 7, for 15 minutes, or until the mushrooms are tender. Split and lightly toast 4 ciabatta rolls. Place a mushroom on the bottom half of each roll, then divide 50 g (2 oz) soft goats' cheese, 4 tablespoons shop-bought fresh green pesto and 1 thinly sliced tomato among them. Replace the tops of the rolls and serve the burgers with a rocket salad.

AFFORDABILITY
1

SPICY PANEER
WITH TOMATOES, PEAS & BEANS

1. Heat half the oil in a large frying pan with a lid. Add the paneer, season well with salt and pepper and cook for 3-4 minutes until golden all over. Lift out with a slotted spoon on to a plate.

2. Add the remaining oil and the onion to the pan and cook for 5 mintes, until softened. Stir in the garlic and ginger and cook for a further 1 minute, then add the spices and cook for 30 seconds.

3. Stir in the tomato purée and stock, then add the beans and return the paneer to the pan. Season to taste with salt and pepper, cover and simmer for 5 minutes.

4. Add the peas and tomatoes and cook for a further 3 minutes, then stir in the garam masala. Divide among serving bowls and serve with chapattis.

2 tablespoons vegetable oil
250 g (8 oz) paneer, diced
1 onion, finely chopped
2 garlic cloves, chopped
2 teaspoons finely grated fresh root ginger
1 teaspoon ground coriander
1 teaspoon paprika
1 teaspoon tomato purée
125 ml (4 fl oz) hot vegetable stock (see page 15 for homemade)
150 g (5 oz) French beans, topped and tailed
175 g (6 oz) frozen peas
150 g (5 oz) tomatoes, chopped
1 teaspoon garam masala
salt and pepper
chapattis, to serve

Serves **4**
Prep time **15 minutes**
Cooking time **20 minutes**

AFFORDABILITY

VEGETABLE & TOFU STIR-FRY

Vegan

1 Heat 1 tablespoon of the oil in a wok until starting to smoke, add the tofu and stir-fry over a high heat for 2 minutes, or until golden. Lift out with a slotted spoon on to a plate.

2 Heat the remaining oil in the wok, add the onion and carrots and stir-fry for 1½ minutes. Add the broccoli and red pepper and stir-fry for 1 minute, then add the courgette and sugar snap peas and stir-fry for 1 minute.

3 Combine the soy and chilli sauces and the measured water in a mug, pour into the wok, then return the tofu to the wok and cook for 1 minute. Divide among serving bowls and garnish with the chopped red chillies and basil leaves.

ACCOMPANIMENT TIP

For sesame noodles, to serve as an accompaniment, put 375 g (12 oz) egg thread noodles in a large heatproof bowl, pour over enough boiling water to cover and leave to stand for 4 minutes, or until just tender. Drain well, then toss with 1 tablespoon light soy sauce and 2 teaspoons sesame oil. Serve sprinkled with 1 tablespoon toasted sesame seeds.

3 tablespoons sunflower oil
300 g (10 oz) firm tofu, cubed
1 onion, sliced
2 carrots, sliced
150 g (5 oz) broccoli, broken into small florets and stalks sliced
1 red pepper, cored, deseeded and sliced
1 large courgette, sliced
150 g (5 oz) sugar snap peas
2 tablespoons soy sauce
2 tablespoons sweet chilli sauce
125 ml (4 fl oz) water

To garnish
chopped red chillies
Thai or ordinary basil leaves

Serves **4**
Prep time **10 minutes**
Cooking time **10 minutes**

AFFORDABILITY 1

Okra & Coconut STEW

Vegan

1 Trim the stalk ends from the okra and cut the pods into 1.5 cm (¾ inch) lengths.

2 Heat 2 tablespoons of the oil in a large, deep-sided frying pan with a lid or shallow flameproof casserole and fry the okra for 5 minutes. Lift out with a slotted spoon on to a plate.

3 Add the remaining oil to the pan or casserole and very gently fry the onions, green peppers and celery, stirring frequently, for 10 minutes, or until softened but not browned. Add the garlic, spice blend and turmeric and cook for 1 minute.

4 Pour in the stock and coconut milk and bring to the boil. Reduce the heat, cover and cook gently for 10 minutes. Return the okra to the pan with the sweetcorn, lime juice and coriander and cook for a further 10 minutes. Season to taste with salt and pepper and serve.

ACCOMPANIMENT TIP

For an easy cornbread, to serve as an accompaniment, mix together 150 g (5 oz) cornmeal, 100 g (3½ oz) plain flour, 1 teaspoon salt, 2 teaspoons baking powder, ½ teaspoon ground cumin and ½ teaspoon dried red chilli flakes in a bowl. Beat 1 egg with 200 ml (7 fl oz) milk in a mug, pour into the cornmeal mixture and mix gently until just combined (do not overmix). Turn into a greased 600 ml (1 pint) loaf tin. Bake in a preheated oven, 190°C (375°F), Gas Mark 5, for 30 minutes, or until firm to the touch. Serve warm or transfer to a wire rack to cool.

AFFORDABILITY 1

375 g (12 oz) okra
4 tablespoons vegetable oil
2 onions, chopped
2 green peppers, cored, deseeded and cut into chunks
3 celery sticks, thinly sliced
3 garlic cloves, crushed
4 teaspoons Cajun spice blend
½ teaspoon ground turmeric
300 ml (½ pint) vegetable stock (see page 15 for homemade)
400 ml (14 fl oz) can coconut milk
200 g (7 oz) frozen sweetcorn
juice of 1 lime
4 tablespoons chopped fresh coriander
salt and pepper

Serves **3-4**
Prep time **15 minutes**
Cooking time **40 minutes**

Spiced CHICKPEAS & KALE

Vegan

3 tablespoons vegetable oil
3 red onions, cut into wedges
2 tablespoons mild curry paste
400 g (13 oz) can chopped
    tomatoes
400 g (13 oz) can chickpeas,
    rinsed and drained
300 ml (½ pint) vegetable
    stock (see page 15 for
    homemade)
2 teaspoons soft light brown
    sugar
100 g (3½ oz) kale, tough stalks
    removed
salt and pepper

Serves **4**
Prep time **10 minutes**
Cooking time **35 minutes**

1 Heat the oil in a large saucepan and fry the onions for 5 minutes, or until beginning to colour. Stir in the curry paste and then the tomatoes, chickpeas, stock and sugar. Bring to the boil, then reduce the heat, cover and simmer gently for 20 minutes.

2 Stir in the kale and cook gently for a further 10 minutes. Season to taste with salt and pepper and serve.

ACCOMPANIMENT TIP
For sesame flatbreads, to serve as an accompaniment, place 250 g (8 oz) plain flour, 1 teaspoon salt and 25 g (1 oz) sesame seeds in a bowl. Add 3 tablespoons vegetable oil and 125 ml (4 fl oz) cold water and mix with a round-bladed knife to a dough, adding a dash more water if the dough feels dry. Divide into 8 pieces and very thinly roll out each piece on a lightly floured surface until about 2.5 mm (⅛ inch) thick. Heat a griddle or large dry frying pan until hot and cook the flatbreads for about 2 minutes on each side until pale golden.

AFFORDABILITY **1**

TOMATO & BASIL TART

butter for greasing
375 g (12 oz) ready-made puff
  pastry
plain flour, for dusting
1 egg, beaten
200 g (7 oz) mascarpone
  cheese
50 g (2 oz) Parmesan cheese,
  grated
handful of chopped basil, plus
  extra to garnish
150 g (5 oz) cherry tomatoes,
  halved
1 tablespoon olive oil
salt and pepper

Serves **4**
Prep time **15 minutes**
Cooking time **20-25 minutes**

1 Lightly grease a baking sheet with butter. Roll out the
pastry to a 30 cm (12 inch) disc. Place on the prepared
baking sheet and roll the edges up to create a 1 cm
(½ inch) border. Press the border down with your thumb
to make a crumpled edge, then prick over the middle
of the pastry disc a few times with a fork. Place in the
freezer for a few minutes.

2 Brush the border of the pastry with a little of the beaten
egg. Mix together the mascarpone, remaining egg,
Parmesan and basil in a bowl, season to taste with salt
and pepper and spread over the centre of the tart.
Arrange the tomatoes on top of the tart and drizzle
over the oil. Bake in a preheated oven, 220°C (425°F),
Gas Mark 7, for 20-25 minutes until golden and crisp.

MAD ABOUT MAINS

ROAST CHICKEN WITH BUTTERNUT SQUASH

PAELLA

CHICKEN WITH SPRING HERBS

BEEF & PICKLED ONION STEW

Salmon
WITH GREEN VEGETABLES

1 tablespoon olive oil
1 leek, trimmed, cleaned and thinly sliced
275 ml (9 fl oz) fish stock (see page 104 for homemade)
200 ml (7 fl oz) crème fraîche
125 g (4 oz) frozen peas
125 g (4 oz) frozen soya or broad beans
4 chunky skinless salmon fillets, about 150 g (5 oz) each
2 tablespoons snipped chives
pepper
mashed potato, to serve

....

Serves **4**
Prep time **5 minutes**
Cooking time **20 minutes**

....

1 Heat the oil in a large heavy-based frying pan with a lid and cook the leek over a medium heat, stirring frequently, for 3 minutes, or until softened. Pour in the stock, bring to the boil and continue boiling for 2 minutes or until reduced a little.

2 Add the crème fraîche and stir well to mix. Add the peas, soya or broad beans and salmon and return to the boil. Reduce the heat, cover and simmer for 10 minutes, or until the fish is opaque and cooked through and the peas and beans are piping hot.

3 Sprinkle over the chives, season with pepper and serve spooned over instant mashed potato.

VARIATION
For creamy salmon and green vegetables, melt 1 tablespoon butter in a heavy-based frying pan and cook 2 skinless salmon fillets, about 150 g (5 oz) each, cut into small cubes, and 50 g (2 oz) frozen peas over a medium heat, stirring gently, for 3 minutes. Add 16 thin asparagus spears, trimmed and chopped into 3.5 cm (1½ inch) pieces, pour in 75 ml (3 fl oz) fish stock and 275 ml (9 fl oz) single cream and cook gently for a further 5 minutes. Garnish with torn basil or parsley leaves and serve with cooked pasta.

CHICKEN, HAM & CABBAGE STEW

1 Drain the beans and transfer to a large saucepan. Cover with fresh cold water and bring to the boil. Reduce the heat and simmer for 40 minutes, or until just tender. Drain and set aside.

2 Add the drained ham to the empty bean pan with the chicken legs, onions and bay leaves. Pour over the measured water and bring to a gentle simmer. Cover and cook very gently for 1 hour.

3 Cut the potatoes into small chunks and add to the pan with the beans and paprika. Cook very gently, covered, for a further 20 minutes, or until the potatoes are tender.

4 Lift the chicken and ham from the pan with a slotted spoon and transfer to a plate. Once cool enough to handle, pull the meat from the bones, discarding the skin. Shred or chop all the meat into small pieces.

5 Return the meat to the pan. Stir in the cabbage and coriander and heat through gently. Season with pepper and serve.

150 g (5 oz) dried haricot beans, soaked in a bowl of cold water overnight
1 ham hock or gammon joint, about 750 g (1½ lb), soaked in a bowl of cold water overnight
4 chicken legs
2 onions, chopped
3 bay leaves
1.2 litres (2 pints) cold water
500 g (1 lb) floury potatoes
1 tablespoon paprika
200 g (7 oz) green cabbage, shredded
15 g (½ oz) fresh coriander, roughly chopped
pepper

Serves **6**
Prep time **30 minutes, plus overnight soaking**
Cooking time **2 hours 10 minutes**

Lemon chilli
CHICKEN

AFFORDABILITY
2

1 chicken, about 1.75 kg (3½ lb), jointed
8 garlic cloves, peeled
4 juicy lemons, quartered and squeezed, skins reserved
1 small red chilli, deseeded and chopped
2 tablespoons orange blossom honey
4 tablespoons chopped parsley, plus sprigs to garnish
salt and pepper

Serves **4**
Prep time **25 minutes, plus marinating**
Cooking time **45 minutes**

1 Arrange the chicken pieces in a shallow, flameproof casserole. Crush 2 of the garlic cloves, then put them in a mug with the lemon juice, chilli and honey and stir well. Pour the mixture over the chicken. Tuck the lemon skins around the meat, cover with clingfilm and leave to marinate in the refrigerator for at least 2 hours or overnight, turning once or twice.

2 Turn the chicken pieces skin-side up, scatter over the remaining whole garlic cloves and place the lemon skins, cut-side down, on top. Cook the chicken in a preheated oven, 200°C (400°F), Gas Mark 6, for 45 minutes, or until golden brown, cooked through and tender. Stir in the parsley, season to taste with salt and pepper and serve garnished with sprigs of parsley.

STUDENT TIP

It's cheaper to buy a whole chicken and cut it into portions. You could ask the butcher to do this for you or, if you have a good-quality sharp knife, you could do it yourself. It's simply a case of cutting the chicken in half, then separating the legs from the breast and cutting the legs from the thighs — this will give you six portions ready for the pot.

CHICKEN
with *Spring Herbs*

250 g (8 oz) mascarpone cheese
1 handful of chervil, finely chopped
½ bunch of parsley, finely chopped
2 tablespoons chopped mint
4 boneless, skin-on chicken breasts
25 g (1 oz) butter
200 ml (7 fl oz) white wine
salt and pepper
garlic bread, to serve (optional)

Serves **4**
Prep time **15 minutes**
Cooking time **25 minutes**

1 Mix together the mascarpone and herbs in a bowl and season well with salt and pepper. Lift the skin away from each chicken breast and spread a quarter of the mascarpone mixture on each breast. Replace the skin and smooth carefully over the mascarpone mixture. Season with salt and pepper.

2 Place the chicken breasts in a baking dish, dot with the butter and pour the wine around it. Roast the chicken in a preheated oven, 180°C (350°F), Gas Mark 4, for 20-25 minutes until golden and crisp and cooked through. Serve with garlic bread, if liked.

AFFORDABILITY

CHICKEN, CHORIZO & BLACK BEAN STEW

250 g (8 oz) dried black beans, soaked in a bowl of cold water overnight
8 bone-in, skinless chicken thighs
150 g (5 oz) chorizo sausage, cut into small chunks
1 onion, sliced
1 fennel bulb, trimmed and chopped
2 green peppers, cored, deseeded and cut into chunks
1 teaspoon saffron threads
salt and pepper

Serves **4-5**
Prep time **15 minutes, plus overnight soaking**
Cooking time **2½ hours**

1 Drain the beans and transfer to a large flameproof casserole. Cover with plenty of fresh cold water. Bring to the boil and boil for 10 minutes. Drain the beans and return to the pan.

2 Add the chicken, chorizo, onion, fennel and green peppers and sprinkle in the saffron. Almost cover the ingredients with cold water and bring to a simmer. Cover and cook in a preheated oven, 160°C (325°F), Gas Mark 3, for 2 hours, or until the beans are very soft.

3 Using a slotted spoon, drain a couple of spoonfuls of the beans and transfer them to a bowl. Mash the beans with a fork and then return to the casserole, stirring gently to thicken the juices. Season to taste with salt and pepper and serve.

VARIATION

For chorizo with chickpeas, fry 150 g (5 oz) diced chorizo sausage in a large saucepan. Add 2 thinly sliced shallots, 2 x 400 g (13 oz) cans chopped tomatoes, 2 x 400 g (13 oz) cans chickpeas, rinsed and drained, 40 g (1½ oz) raisins, 2 tablespoons sherry vinegar, 1 tablespoon clear honey and 1 teaspoon paprika. Bring to a simmer, then reduce the heat, cover and cook gently for 30 minutes. Season to taste with salt and pepper and serve.

AFFORDABILITY 2

ROAST CHICKEN WITH
BUTTERNUT SQUASH

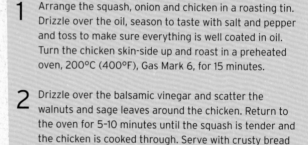

500 g (1 lb) butternut squash, peeled, deseeded and cut into thin slices

1 red onion, sliced

4 bone-in, skin-on chicken breasts

2 tablespoons olive oil

1 tablespoon balsamic vinegar

25 g (1 oz) walnut halves

8 sage leaves

salt and pepper

To serve

crusty bread

green salad

Serves **4**

Prep time **10 minutes**

Cooking time **20-25 minutes**

1 Arrange the squash, onion and chicken in a roasting tin. Drizzle over the oil, season to taste with salt and pepper and toss to make sure everything is well coated in oil. Turn the chicken skin-side up and roast in a preheated oven, 200°C (400°F), Gas Mark 6, for 15 minutes.

2 Drizzle over the balsamic vinegar and scatter the walnuts and sage leaves around the chicken. Return to the oven for 5-10 minutes until the squash is tender and the chicken is cooked through. Serve with crusty bread and green salad.

VARIATION

For a chicken, butternut squash and goats' cheese pasta, cook 250 g (8 oz) peeled, deseeded and diced butternut squash in a large saucepan of lightly salted boiling water for 6 minutes. Add 500 g (1 lb) fresh penne pasta and cook for a further 3 minutes, or according to the packet instructions. Add 150 g (5 oz) baby spinach leaves, then drain immediately and return the pasta and vegetables to the pan. Stir in 75 g (3 oz) soft goats' cheese and 1 ready-cooked chicken breast, torn into shreds, then season to taste with salt and pepper and serve topped with roughly chopped walnuts.

AFFORDABILITY

Chicken RATATOUILLE

1 Cut a couple of slashes across each chicken thigh and season with salt and pepper. Heat the oil in a large, deep frying pan, add the chicken and cook over a high heat for 5 minutes, turning occasionally.

2 Add the onion, aubergine, green and red peppers, courgettes and garlic and cook for 10 minutes, or until softened, adding a little water if the mixture becomes too dry.

3 Pour in the tomatoes, add the sugar, and season to taste with salt and pepper. Bring to the boil, stirring, then reduce the heat, cover and simmer for 15 minutes, stirring occasionally. Stir in the basil and serve.

8 small skinless chicken thighs
1 tablespoon olive oil
1 onion, chopped
1 aubergine, cut into bite-sized chunks
1 green pepper, cored, deseeded and cut into bite-sized chunks
1 red pepper, cored, deseeded and cut into bite-sized chunks
2 courgettes, chopped
1 garlic clove, crushed
400 g (13 oz) can chopped tomatoes
pinch of caster sugar
handful of basil leaves, roughly torn
salt and pepper

Serves **4**
Prep time **15 minutes**
Cooking time **30 minutes**

AFFORDABILITY

PAPRIKA CHICKEN & PEPPERS

AFFORDABILITY 1

1 Heat the oil in a large frying pan, add the chicken and stir-fry over a high heat for 5 minutes. Add the garlic paste, paprika, mixed peppers and tomato purée and cook, stirring, for 3 minutes.

2 Stir in the soured cream, season to taste with salt and pepper and heat through. Serve with cooked tagliatelle.

1 tablespoon sunflower oil
400 g (13 oz) chicken mini-fillets
1 teaspoon garlic paste
1 tablespoon paprika
175 g (6 oz) frozen sliced mixed peppers
1 tablespoon tomato purée
150 ml (¼ pint) soured cream
salt and pepper
cooked tagliatelle, to serve

Serves **4**
Prep time **5 minutes**
Cooking time **10 minutes**

STUDENT TIP

Always label your freezer food clearly… unless you don't mind having a lucky dip dinner in a couple of weeks' time. Buy a batch of freezer bags, stickers and a suitable marker pen and keep them somewhere handy so you can batch up leftovers quickly.

Tandoori CHICKEN
& ONIONS

1 Line a baking sheet with foil and set a wire rack on top. Make 3 slashes across each chicken breast. Mix together the yogurt, garlic, ginger and tandoori paste in a bowl and season well with salt and pepper. Add the chicken and rub the tandoori mixture all over the chicken. Leave to marinate for 5-10 minutes.

2 Toss the chicken with the onion and oil, then arrange on the rack. Bake in a preheated oven, 230°C (450°F), Gas Mark 8, for 7 minutes.

3 Add the tomatoes, scatter over the butter and return to the oven for a further 5-10 minutes until the chicken is charred and cooked through. Serve with lime wedges, raita and warm naan breads.

4 skinless chicken breast fillets
100 ml (3½ fl oz) natural yogurt
1 garlic clove, crushed
2 teaspoons finely grated fresh root ginger
2 tablespoons tandoori curry paste
1 onion, cut into wedges
2 tablespoons vegetable oil
2 tomatoes, quartered
15 g (½ oz) butter, cut into small pieces
salt and pepper

To serve
lime wedges
ready-made raita
warm naan breads

Serves **4**
Prep time **10 minutes, plus marinating**
Cooking time **15-20 minutes**

Chicken & tomato
POLENTA PIE

2 tablespoons olive oil
300 g (10 oz) skinless chicken
   breast fillets, diced
2 garlic cloves, finely chopped
400 g (13 oz) can chopped
   tomatoes
1 teaspoon tomato purée
pinch of dried chilli flakes
handful of chopped basil
1 courgette, sliced
500 g (1 lb) ready-cooked
   polenta, cut into 1 cm (½ inch)
   slices
25 g (1 oz) Parmesan cheese,
   grated
salt and pepper

Serves **4**
Prep time **10 minutes**
Cooking time **30-35 minutes**

1 Heat the oil in a shallow flameproof casserole. Add the chicken, season to taste with salt and pepper and cook for 3-4 minutes until starting to turn golden. Lift out with a slotted spoon on to a plate.

2 Add the garlic to the casserole and cook for 1 minute, then pour in the tomatoes and stir in the tomato purée, chilli flakes and basil. Bring to the boil, then reduce the heat and simmer for 10 minutes.

3 Return the chicken to the casserole, add the courgette and cook for a further 5-10 minutes until the chicken is cooked through.

4 Arrange the polenta slices on top of the chicken mixture, then scatter over the Parmesan. Cook under a preheated hot grill for 5 minutes, or until golden and bubbling.

Herby roast
TURKEY BREAST

handful of chopped rosemary
handful of chopped parsley
25 g (1 oz) butter, softened
800 g (1 lb 10 oz) turkey breast
    joint
6 garlic cloves
50 ml (2 fl oz) dry white wine
50 ml (2 fl oz) hot chicken stock
    (see page 11 for homemade)
4 slices of pancetta
2 x 400 g (13 oz) cans butter
    beans, rinsed and drained
handful of sun-blush tomatoes,
    roughly chopped
50 ml (2 fl oz) double cream
salt and pepper

Serves **4**
Prep time **10 minutes**
Cooking time **30 minutes**

1 Mix together the rosemary, three-quarters of the parsley and the butter in a bowl. Smear the flavoured butter over the turkey joint. Season to taste with salt and pepper.

2 Place the turkey in a roasting tin with the whole garlic cloves, pour the wine and stock into the tin and arrange the pancetta on top of the turkey. Roast in a preheated oven, 220°C (425°F), Gas Mark 7, for 25 minutes.

3 Add the beans, tomatoes and cream to the roasting tin, topping up with a little water if necessary. Season to taste with salt and pepper, then return to the oven for a further 3–5 minutes until the turkey is cooked through and the beans are warm.

4 Cut the turkey into slices and arrange on serving plates with the crispy pancetta and the beans, sprinkled with the remaining parsley.

VARIATION

For spaghetti with turkey, ham and beans, cook 500 g (1 lb) fresh spaghetti in a large saucepan of lightly salted boiling water according to the packet instructions. Add 200 g (7 oz) canned cannellini beans, rinsed and drained, for the last minute of the cooking time. Drain and then return the pasta and beans to the pan. Add 4 slices of ready-cooked turkey, cut into strips, 2 slices of ham, cut into strips, and a handful of chopped sun-blush tomatoes. Stir in 4 tablespoons crème fraîche and 50 g 2 oz) rocket. To serve, divide among serving plates and sprinkle over plenty of grated Parmesan cheese.

TURKEY, SWEET POTATO & COCONUT CURRY

1. Heat the oil in a large, shallow saucepan or frying pan. Add the fennel and onion and fry gently, stirring frequently, for 5 minutes. Add the turkey and garlic and fry for a further 5 minutes, or until the ingredients are beginning to lightly brown.

2. Stir in the stock, oregano or thyme, sun-dried tomato paste or tomato purée and sweet potatoes. Bring to a gentle simmer, cover and cook for 15 minutes.

3. Add the creamed coconut and jalapeño peppers to the pan. The coconut will melt into the juices. Cover and cook for a further 25 minutes, stirring occasionally, until the potatoes are tender. Add a dash of water towards the end of the cooking time if the sauce starts to dry out.

4. Season to taste with salt, if necessary. Serve in bowls, sprinkled with chopped coriander.

COOKING TIP
The fresh coriander adds another burst of flavour to the curry. To save wasting the rest of the pack, roughly chop the coriander and freeze in a small polythene bag for another time.

2 tablespoons vegetable oil
1 fennel bulb, chopped
1 red onion, chopped
350 g (11½ oz) lean turkey breast, cut into small chunks
4 garlic cloves, finely chopped
500 ml (17 fl oz) chicken or vegetable stock (see pages 11 or 15 for homemade)
1 teaspoon dried oregano or thyme
2 tablespoons sun-dried tomato paste or tomato purée
750 g (1½ lb) sweet potatoes, scrubbed and cut into 2 cm (¾ inch) chunks
100 g (3½ oz) creamed coconut, cut into a few pieces
30 g (1¼ oz) jalapeño peppers in brine, drained and chopped
salt
chopped fresh coriander, to garnish

Serves **4**
Prep time **20 minutes**
Cooking time **50 minutes**

AFFORDABILITY 2

PORK & LEEK *stew*

1 Season the pork with plenty of salt and pepper. Heat 1 tablespoon of the oil in a large flameproof casserole and fry the pork in batches until browned on all sides, lifting out with a slotted spoon on to a plate.

2 Add the remaining oil to the casserole and gently fry the onion and leeks for 5 minutes. Return the pork to the casserole, add the bay leaves and stock and bring to a simmer. Stir in the pearl barley. Cover, reduce the heat to its lowest setting and cook for about 1½ hours until the pork and barley are tender and the cooking juices have thickened.

3 Mix together the flour, suet and a little salt and pepper in a bowl. Add the measured water and mix with a round-bladed knife to a soft dough, adding a dash more water if the mixture feels dry and crumbly, but don't make it too sticky.

4 Stir the prunes into the stew and season to taste with salt and pepper. Using a dessertspoon, place spoonfuls of the dumpling mixture on the surface of the stew, spacing them slightly apart. Re-cover and cook gently for a further 15-20 minutes until the dumplings have risen and have a fluffy texture. Serve in shallow bowls.

1 kg (2 lb) boneless lean pork, diced
2 tablespoons vegetable oil
1 large onion, chopped
500 g (1 lb) leeks, trimmed, cleaned and chopped
3 bay leaves
1.5 litres (2½ pints) chicken or beef stock (see pages 11 or 98 for homemade)
75 g (3 oz) pearl barley
150 g (5 oz) self-raising flour
75 g (3 oz) beef or vegetable suet
about 125 ml (4 fl oz) cold water
150 g (5 oz) stoned prunes, halved
salt and pepper

Serves **4-5**
Prep time **25 minutes**
Cooking time **2 hours**

AFFORDABILITY
2

MEDITERRANEAN
PORK STEW

AFFORDABILITY
2

1 Heat the oil in a flameproof casserole and fry the pork for 4-5 minutes until browned on all sides. Lift out with a slotted spoon on to a plate.

2 Add the onion, garlic and yellow pepper to the casserole and fry for 2 minutes. Return the pork to the casserole together with all the remaining ingredients.

3 Bring to the boil, then reduce the heat, cover and cook gently for 1 hour, or until the meat is tender. Garnish with sprigs of thyme and serve with garlic bread.

VARIATION
For a borlotti bean casserole, omit the pork and fry the onion, garlic and yellow pepper in the oil as above, then stir in the artichoke hearts and tomatoes. Rinse and drain a 400 g (13 oz) can borlotti beans and add to the casserole with the wine, olives, lemon zest and herbs. Bring to the boil, then reduce the heat, cover and cook gently for about 1 hour. Serve garnished with chopped parsley.

1 tablespoon olive oil
250 g (8 oz) boneless lean pork, cut into chunks
1 red onion, cut into thin wedges
1 garlic clove, crushed
1 yellow pepper, cored, deseeded and chopped
8 artichoke hearts in oil, drained and quartered
200 g (7 oz) can chopped tomatoes
100 ml (3½ fl oz) red wine
50 g (2 oz) black olives, pitted
grated zest of 1 lemon
1 bay leaf
1 sprig of thyme, plus extra to garnish
garlic bread, to serve

Serves **2**
Prep time **10 minutes**
Cooking time **1 hour 10 minutes**

LOVELY LEFTOVERS

If the first thing that springs to mind when you think of leftovers is grabbing a slice of congealed pizza from the fridge the morning after a drinking session, think again. Leftover food offers another chance to enjoy a delicious meal; it will make your grocery budget stretch further and it's a great way to make the most of your freezer. If you are freezing your leftovers, make sure you have a stash of freezer bags, ties and labels, or a collection of freezer-proof containers ... and space in the freezer!

One-pot cooking is particularly suited to leftovers, as the food can be easily portioned into containers or freezer bags, labelled and saved for another day. But, while it's quick and easy to simply reheat and serve a portion of a favourite meal, there are also lots of ways to transform your leftovers into a completely new dish. If you are planning to serve up a new incarnation of tonight's dinner, it's very important to cover and chill the leftover food in the refrigerator and to thoroughly reheat or cook it through before its next visit to the dinner table. Here are a few ideas to get you started.

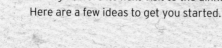

CHILLI CON CARNE

Chilling chilli con carne overnight allows the flavours to really develop and some people would argue that it tastes better the next day. Reheat thoroughly and use as a filling for baked potatoes or roasted peppers. It also makes a great pizza topping.

RISOTTO

Crispy, melt-in-the-mouth risotto balls (or arancini to give them their correct Italian name) are the perfect way to use up any risotto that doesn't get devoured on its first outing. Take the leftover risotto from the refrigerator and stir in some chopped mozzarella, if you like. Dip the risotto balls in beaten egg and then roll them in breadcrumbs. Heat vegetable oil in a large pan and cook the balls until they've turned an even golden brown.

CHICKEN

This is probably the most versatile one-pot leftover ingredient. Slice pot-roast chicken and use it as a filling for sandwiches and wraps; add it to pasta sauces or salads; make a chicken pie with ham and leeks or use chicken thighs for a curry or a risotto.

PORK CHOPS
& POTATOES

2 tablespoons olive oil
4 large pork chops, about 250 g
   (8 oz) each
125 g (4 oz) smoked bacon in
   one piece, rind discarded, and
   diced
1 large onion, sliced
750 g (1½ lb) potatoes, cut into
   2.5 cm (1 inch) cubes
2 garlic cloves, chopped
2 teaspoons dried oregano
grated zest and juice of 1 lemon
250 ml (8 fl oz) chicken stock
   (see page 11 for homemade)
salt and pepper
thyme leaves, to garnish
   (optional)

Serves **4**
Prep time **10 minutes**
Cooking time **50 minutes**

1   Heat the oil in a flameproof casserole and fry the pork
    chops until browned on both sides. Lift out with a slotted
    spoon on to a plate.

2   Add the bacon and onion to the casserole and cook over
    a medium heat, stirring, for 3-4 minutes until golden.

3   Stir the potatoes, garlic, oregano and lemon zest into
    the casserole. Pour over the stock and lemon juice and
    season lightly with salt and pepper. Cook, uncovered,
    in a preheated oven, 180°C (350°F), Gas Mark 4, for
    20 minutes.

4   Arrange the chops on top of the potato mixture and
    return to the oven for a further 20 minutes, or until the
    potatoes and pork chops are cooked through. Serve
    garnished with thyme leaves, if liked.

VARIATION
For pork chops with
sweet potatoes and
sage, cook the recipe
above using 750 g
(1½ lb) sweet potatoes,
peeled and cut into
cubes, instead of
the potatoes and
1 tablespoon chopped
sage in place of the
dried oregano.

AFFORDABILITY
2

HOISIN PORK *Stir-fry*

1 tablespoon hoisin sauce
1 tablespoon light soy sauce
1 tablespoon white wine
 vinegar
1 tablespoon vegetable oil
2 garlic cloves, sliced
1 teaspoon grated fresh root
 ginger
1 small red chilli, deseeded and
 sliced
250 g (8 oz) pork fillet, thinly
 sliced
175 g (6 oz) sugar snap peas
175 g (6 oz) broccoli florets
2 tablespoons water
steamed rice, to serve

Serves **2**
Prep time **10 minutes**
Cooking time **10 minutes**

1 Combine the hoisin and soy sauces and vinegar in
a mug and set aside.

2 Heat the oil in a wok until starting to smoke, add the
garlic, ginger and chilli and stir-fry over a high heat
for 10 seconds. Add the pork fillet and stir-fry for
2–3 minutes, or until golden. Lift out with a slotted
spoon on to a plate.

3 Add the sugar snap peas and broccoli florets to the
wok and stir-fry for 1 minute. Add the measured water
and cook for a further 1 minute.

4 Return the pork to the wok, add the hoisin mixture and
cook for 1 minute, or until the vegetables are cooked.
Serve with steamed rice.

VARIATION
For roasted hoisin pork, make the hoisin mixture as above.
Brush the sauce over 4 pieces of pork fillet, about 175 g
(6 oz) each, in a roasting tin and roast in a preheated
oven, 200°C (400°F), Gas Mark 6, for 15 minutes. Leave
to rest for 5 minutes, then serve with steamed green
vegetables and boiled rice.

AFFORDABILITY
2

SAUSAGE & ONION
TRAYBAKE

3 red onions, cut into wedges

3 red apples, cored and cut into
6 wedges

200 g (7 oz) baby carrots,
scrubbed

3 potatoes, peeled and cut into
small cubes

4 tablespoons olive oil

12 good-quality pork sausages

2 tablespoons chopped sage

1 tablespoon rosemary

3 tablespoons clear honey

salt and pepper

Serves **4**
Prep time **10 minutes**
Cooking time **20-25 minutes**

1 Scatter the onions, apples, carrots and potatoes in
a large roasting tin. Drizzle over the oil and toss well
to lightly coat all the vegetables in the oil. Season
generously with salt and pepper. Arrange the sausages
in and around the vegetables, sprinkle over the herbs
and toss again.

2 Bake in a preheated oven, 200°C (400°F), Gas Mark 6,
for 20-22 minutes until golden and cooked through.

3 Remove from the oven and drizzle over the honey. Toss
all the vegetables and sausages in the honey and serve.

VARIATION

For a quick pork, apple and onion stir-fry, cut 250 g (8 oz)
pork fillet into very thin slices. Heat 2 tablespoons olive oil
in a large wok or heavy-based frying pan and stir-fry the
pork over a high heat for 2-3 minutes. Add 2 cored apples
and 2 red onions, each cut into slim wedges, and stir-fry
for 3-4 minutes until browned and softened. Add 1 tablespoon
chopped sage leaves or rosemary and toss to mix. Serve
with warm ciabatta and plenty of Dijon mustard.

AFFORDABILITY

1

CHORIZO & CAULIFLOWER CHEESE PIE

1. Layer up half the cauliflower, onion, chorizo and parsnips in a pie dish or shallow ovenproof dish. Repeat with the remaining cauliflower, onion, chorizo and parsnips and season with pepper – you probably won't need any salt. Spoon the cheese sauce on top.

2. Roll out the pastry until large enough to generously cover the top of the dish. (If the pastry sticks to the surface, dust with a sprinkling of flour). Brush the edges of the dish with water and position the pastry, pressing it firmly down on the rim of the dish. Trim off the excess, leaving a bit of an overhang as the pastry will shrink slightly as it cooks.

3. Make a hole in the centre of the pie with the tip of a knife to allow the steam to escape. Decorate by pressing a fork all around the edges of the pie or by crimping the edges between your thumb and fingers.

4. Brush the top of the pie with beaten egg or milk to glaze (use your fingers or a piece of kitchen paper if you don't have a pastry brush). If liked, decorate the top of the pie with the pastry trimmings.

5. Bake in a preheated oven, 200°C (400°F), Gas Mark 6, for about 1 hour or until the pastry is risen and golden and the vegetables feel tender when you press the tip of a knife down into the filling. Cover the pie with foil if it starts to over-brown before it's cooked through. Serve with seasonal green vegetables.

VARIATION

For a vegetarian version, omit the chorizo and sprinkle the vegetables with a finely chopped red chilli before adding the cheese sauce. Alternatively, try a sprinkling of cumin seeds and a generous sprinkling of chopped fresh coriander.

---

1 cauliflower, cut into small pieces
1 large red onion, thinly sliced
125 g (4 oz) chorizo sausage, cut into 1 cm (½ inch) dice
2 parsnips, thinly sliced
250 g (8 oz) tub ready-made cheese sauce
500 g (1 lb) puff pastry
pepper
beaten egg or milk, to glaze
seasonal green vegetables, to serve

Serves **4**
Prep time **20 minutes**
Cooking time **1 hour**

AFFORDABILITY 2

CHORIZO & CHICKPEA STEW

1 teaspoon olive oil
2 red onions, chopped
2 red peppers, cored, deseeded
  and chopped
100 g (3½ oz) chorizo sausage,
  thinly sliced
500 g (1 lb) cooked new
  potatoes, sliced
500 g (1 lb) plum tomatoes,
  chopped, or 400 g (13 oz) can
  chopped tomatoes, drained
400 g (13 oz) can chickpeas,
  rinsed and drained
2 tablespoons chopped parsley,
  to garnish
garlic bread, to serve

Serves **4**
Prep time **5 minutes**
Cooking time **20 minutes**

1 Heat the oil in a large frying pan and fry the onions and red peppers over a medium heat for 3-4 minutes. Add the chorizo and cook, turning frequently, for 2 minutes.

2 Stir the potatoes, tomatoes and chickpeas into the pan and bring to the boil. Reduce the heat and cook gently for 10 minutes. Garnish with the chopped parsley and serve with garlic bread to mop up all the juices.

VARIATION
For a sausage and mixed bean stew, fry the onions and red peppers in the oil as above. Add 4 pork sausages instead of the chorizo to the pan and cook for 4-5 minutes until browned on all sides. Lift the sausages from the pan and cut each into 6 thick slices. Return to the pan and add the potato slices and tomatoes as above but replace the chickpeas with a 400 g (13 oz) can mixed beans, rinsed and drained. Bring to the boil and cook as above. If you prefer a slightly hotter stew, add 1 deseeded and chopped red chilli when frying the onions and peppers.

AFFORDABILITY
1

PORK, APPLE &
Mustard

2 tablespoons olive oil
25 g (1 oz) butter
1 large red onion, cut into slim
    wedges
2 red apples, cored and cut into
    slim wedges
600 g (1 lb 3 oz) pork fillet,
    thinly sliced
300 ml (½ pint) hot chicken
    stock (see page 11 for
    homemade)
200 ml (7 fl oz) crème fraîche
2 tablespoons Dijon mustard
2 tablespoons wholegrain
    mustard
6 tablespoons chopped parsley
mashed potatoes, to serve

Serves **4-6**
Prep time **10 minutes**
Cooking time **20 minutes**

AFFORDABILITY
2

1   Heat the oil and butter in a large frying pan, add the
onion and apples and cook over a medium-high heat for
5 minutes, turning and stirring occasionally, until golden
and starting to soften. Lift out with a slotted spoon on
to a plate.

2   Add the pork to the pan and cook over a high heat for
5 minutes, or until golden and cooked through. Return the
onion and apples to the pan with the stock and bring to
the boil. Reduce the heat and simmer for 3 minutes, or
until the stock has reduced by half, then add the crème
fraîche and mustards and heat through for 2 minutes.
Stir in the parsley, then serve hot with mashed potatoes.

SWEET & SOUR PORK

1 tablespoon vegetable oil
½ pineapple, skinned, cored
  and cut into bite-sized chunks
1 onion, cut into chunks
1 orange pepper, cored,
  deseeded and cut into chunks
375 g (12 oz) pork fillet, cut into
  strips
100 g (3½ oz) mangetout,
  halved lengthways
6 tablespoons tomato ketchup
2 tablespoons soft light brown
  sugar
2 tablespoons white wine or
  malt vinegar
cooked egg noodles, to serve
  (optional)

Serves **4**
Prep time **10 minutes**
Cooking time **20 minutes**

1 Heat the oil in a large wok and stir-fry the pineapple over a very high heat for 3-4 minutes until browned in places. Lift out with a slotted spoon on to a plate.

2 Add the onion and orange pepper to the wok and cook over a high heat, stirring frequently, for 5 minutes, or until softened. Add the pork and stir-fry for 5 minutes, or until browned and cooked through.

3 Return the pineapple to the wok together with the mangetout and cook, stirring occasionally, for 2 minutes.

4 Meanwhile, mix together the tomato ketchup, sugar and vinegar in a mug. Pour over the pork mixture, toss and cook for a further 1 minute to heat the sauce through. Serve immediately, with cooked egg noodles, if liked.

AFFORDABILITY 2

Liver & ONIONS

50 g (2 oz) butter
2 tablespoons olive oil
2 large onions, thinly sliced
625 g (1¼ lb) calves' liver, thinly sliced (ask your butcher to slice as thinly as possible)
2 tablespoons finely chopped parsley, to garnish
salt and pepper

Serves **4**
Prep time **10 minutes**
Cooking time **40-45 minutes**

1 Melt half the butter with the oil in a large heavy-based frying pan with a tight-fitting lid. Add the onions and season with salt and pepper, then cover, reduce the heat to its lowest setting and cook, stirring occasionally, for 35-40 minutes until very soft and golden. Lift out with a slotted spoon on to a plate.

2 Increase the heat to high and melt the remaining butter in the pan. Season the liver with salt and pepper. Once the butter starts foaming, add the liver and cook for 1-2 minutes until browned. Turn over the liver, return the onions to the pan and cook for a further 1 minute. Serve garnished with the chopped parsley.

AFFORDABILITY
1

CELERIAC & BACON BAKE

1 Cut away the skin from the celeriac until you have about 600 g (1 lb 3 oz) of flesh. Cut the flesh into manageable pieces, about the size of the potatoes. Slice the celeriac and potatoes as thinly as possible.

2 Layer up half the celeriac and potatoes in a shallow ovenproof dish, seasoning lightly with pepper as you go. Arrange the bacon and onion on top. Sprinkle with half the Cheddar then layer up the remaining celeriac and potatoes.

3 Pour over the stock, then the cream and sprinkle with the remaining Cheddar. Cover with foil and bake in a preheated oven, 180°C (350°F), Gas Mark 4, for 30 minutes. Remove the foil and bake for a further 45 minutes, or until the surface is bubbling and golden and the vegetables are tender. Serve with a mixed leaf salad.

1 small celeriac, about 750 g (1½ lb)
300 g (10 oz) baking potatoes
100 g (3½ oz) smoked streaky bacon, diced
1 large onion, chopped
250 g (8 oz) Cheddar cheese, grated
150 ml (¼ pint) chicken or vegetable stock (see pages 11 or 15 for homemade)
200 ml (7 fl oz) double cream
pepper
mixed leaf salad, to serve

Serves **4**
Prep time **25 minutes**
Cooking time **1¼ hours**

BACON, PEA & COURGETTE *Risotto*

50 g (2 oz) butter
150 g (5 oz) streaky bacon, diced
300 g (10 oz) risotto rice
100 ml (3½ fl oz) dry white wine (optional)
900 ml (1½ pints) hot chicken or vegetable stock (see pages 11 or 15 for homemade) (add an extra 100 ml/3½ fl oz if not using wine)
2 courgettes, about 325 g (11 oz) in total, coarsely grated
200 g (7 oz) frozen peas, defrosted
1 small bunch of basil, shredded (optional)
salt and pepper
grated Parmesan cheese, to serve

Serves **4**
Prep time **5 minutes**
Cooking time **30 minutes**

1 Melt the butter in a large frying pan or saucepan and cook the bacon over a medium heat for 6-7 minutes until golden. Lift out half of the bacon with a slotted spoon on to a plate.

2 Add the rice to the pan and stir well. Pour in the wine, if using, and stock. Bring to the boil, then simmer gently for 15-18 minutes, stirring as often as possible, until the rice is tender and creamy. Stir in the courgette and peas for the final 2-3 minutes of the cooking time.

3 Season with salt and pepper, then spoon the risotto into 4 serving bowls. Scatter over the reserved bacon and the basil, if using. Serve sprinkled with grated Parmesan.

Spicy SAUSAGE & TOMATO

1 Heat the oil in a large frying pan, add the sausages and fry over a high heat for 3-4 minutes until browned. Add the chilli, garlic, onion and chilli flakes and fry for a further 1-2 minutes.

2 Stir in the tomatoes, sugar and rosemary and bring to the boil, then reduce the heat to medium and cook for 8-10 minutes. Season with salt and pepper. Garnish with the chopped parsley, then serve with cooked pasta and grated Parmesan to sprinkle over.

2 tablespoons olive oil
8 thick, spicy Italian sausages, cut into 2 cm (¾ inch) pieces
1 red chilli, deseeded and finely chopped
4 garlic cloves, finely chopped
1 onion, finely chopped
1 teaspoon dried red chilli flakes
400 g (13 oz) can chopped tomatoes with herbs
1 teaspoon caster sugar
2 teaspoons chopped rosemary
salt and pepper
4 tablespoons chopped parsley, to garnish

To serve
cooked pasta, such as penne
100 g (3½ oz) Parmesan cheese, grated

Serves **4**
Prep time **10 minutes**
Cooking time **20 minutes**

SEARED PORK CHOPS
WITH CHILLI CORN

1 Heat 1 tablespoon of the oil in a large frying pan.
Season the chops to taste with salt and pepper and
cook in the pan for 5-7 minutes on each side until
golden and cooked through. Remove from the pan
and keep warm while you cook the chilli corn.

2 Add the remaining oil to the pan, followed by the
sweetcorn. Cook for 2 minutes, or until starting to
brown, then stir in the spring onions and chilli and
cook for a further 1 minute. Stir in the crème fraîche
and lime zest and season to taste with salt and pepper.
Scatter over the chopped coriander and serve with
the pork chops.

VARIATION
For ham and corn melts, spread 100 g (3½ oz) cream
cheese over 4 wheat tortillas. Tear up 4 slices of ham
and scatter on top with 75 g (3 oz) canned sweetcorn
kernels and 25 g (1 oz) grated Cheddar cheese. Place
another tortilla on top of each, then cook under a
preheated hot grill for 3 minutes. Carefully turn over
and cook for a further 2-3 minutes until the cheese
has melted inside.

2 tablespoons olive oil
4 pork chops
200 g (7 oz) fresh or canned
   sweetcorn kernels
2 spring onions, thinly sliced
1 red chilli, chopped
5 tablespoons crème fraîche
finely grated zest of 1 lime
salt and pepper
handful of chopped fresh
   coriander, to garnish

Serves **4**
Prep time **5 minutes**
Cooking time **15-20 minutes**

BEEF & PICKLED ONION *Stew*

3 tablespoons plain flour
1 kg (2 lb) braising steak, cut
  into large chunks
2 tablespoons olive oil
500 g (1 lb) jar pickled onions,
  drained
2 carrots, thickly sliced
300 ml (½ pint) beer
600 ml (1 pint) beef stock (see
  page 98 for homemade)
4 tablespoons tomato purée
1 tablespoon Worcestershire
  sauce
2 bay leaves
salt and pepper
chopped parsley, to garnish

Serves **4**
Prep time **10 minutes**
Cooking time **2¼ hours**

1 Season the flour with salt and pepper on a plate.
  Coat the beef with the flour.

2 Heat the oil in a large flameproof casserole and fry
  the beef in batches until browned on all sides, lifting
  out with a slotted spoon on to a plate.

3 Return all the beef to the casserole. Stir in the pickled
  onions and carrots, then gradually blend in the beer
  and stock. Bring to the boil, stirring, then add the tomato
  purée, Worcestershire sauce, and bay leaves and season
  with salt and pepper to taste.

4 Cover and cook in a preheated oven, 160°C (325°F),
  Gas Mark 3, for 2 hours, stirring halfway through, until
  the beef and vegetables are tender. Garnish with the
  chopped parsley and serve immediately.

COOKING TIP
If you don't have a flameproof
casserole use a saucepan for frying
off, then transfer to a casserole
or any shallow ovenproof dish.

AFFORDABILITY
2

Beef GOULASH

4 tablespoons olive oil
1.5 kg (3 lb) braising steak, cut into large chunks
2 onions, sliced
2 red peppers, cored, deseeded and diced
1 tablespoon smoked paprika
2 tablespoons chopped marjoram
1 teaspoon caraway seeds
1 litre (1¾ pints) beef stock (see tip for homemade)
5 tablespoons tomato purée
salt and pepper
French bread, to serve

Serves **8**
Prep time **10 minutes**
Cooking time **2–2½ hours**

1 Heat the oil in a flameproof casserole and fry the beef in batches until browned on all sides, lifting out with a slotted spoon on to a plate.

2 Add the onions and red peppers to the casserole and cook gently for 10 minutes, or until softened. Stir in the paprika, marjoram and caraway seeds and cook, stirring, for 1 minute.

3 Return the beef to the casserole. Add the stock and tomato purée, season to taste with salt and pepper and bring to the boil, stirring. Reduce the heat, cover and cook gently for 1½–2 hours. If the sauce needs thickening, uncover for the final 30 minutes of the cooking time. Serve with French bread.

COOKING TIP
For a homemade beef stock, place 750 g (1½ lb) shin of beef, cut into chunks, in a large saucepan and add 2 chopped onions, 2–3 chopped carrots, 2 roughly chopped celery sticks, 1 bay leaf, 1 bouquet garni, 4–6 black peppercorns and 1.8 litres (3 pints) cold water. Slowly bring to the boil, then reduce the heat, cover with a well-fitting lid and simmer gently for 2 hours, skimming off any scum that rises to the surface. Strain through a fine sieve, discarding the solids, and leave to cool. Cover and store in the refrigerator for up to several days or freeze for up to 6 months. This makes about 1.5 litres (2½ pints).

AFFORDABILITY
2

BEEF & POTATO
hash

1. Heat 1 tablespoon of the oil in a large heavy-based frying pan with a lid and fry the beef for 10 minutes, breaking up the mince with a wooden spoon and stirring until browned and all the moisture has evaporated. Push the meat to one side of the pan, add the remaining oil, fennel and celery and fry for 5 minutes, or until softened.

2. Blend the cornflour with a little of the stock in a mug, pour into the pan and stir to thicken. Add the remaining stock, tomato purée, potatoes and star anise and bring to a simmer, stirring. Reduce the heat, cover and cook gently for about 30 minutes until the potatoes are tender, stirring occasionally and adding a dash more water if the pan becomes dry.

3. Stir in the soy sauce and sugar and cook for a further 5 minutes, uncovered if necessary to thicken the juices. Season to taste with salt and pepper and stir in the coriander just before serving.

ACCOMPANIMENT TIP
For a watercress salad, to serve as an accompaniment, remove any tough stalks from 100 g (3½ oz) watercress. Peel ½ cucumber, cut in half lengthways, scoop out the seeds and thinly slice the flesh. Put the watercress and cucumber in a large bowl and sprinkle with ½ bunch of spring onions, finely chopped. Whisk 3 tablespoons groundnut or vegetable oil with 2 teaspoons rice vinegar, ½ teaspoon caster sugar and a little salt and pepper in a mug. Drizzle the dressing over the salad.

2 tablespoons vegetable oil
750 g (1½ lb) minced beef
1 fennel bulb, trimmed and chopped
2 celery sticks, chopped
2 teaspoons cornflour
450 ml (¾ pint) beef stock (see page 98 for homemade)
3 tablespoons tomato purée
700 g (1 lb 7 oz) waxy potatoes, cut into 1.5 cm (¾ inch) chunks
4 star anise, broken into pieces and crushed using a pestle and mortar (or a rolling pin or empty wine bottle)
3 tablespoons soy sauce
1 tablespoon light muscovado sugar
15 g (½ oz) roughly chopped fresh coriander
salt and pepper

Serves **4**
Prep time **15 minutes**
Cooking time **50 minutes**

AFFORDABILITY

West Indian
BEEF & BEAN STEW

3 tablespoons sunflower oil
800 g (1 lb 10 oz) minced beef
6 cloves
1 onion, finely chopped
2 tablespoons medium curry
  powder
2 carrots, peeled and cut into
  1 cm (½ inch) cubes
2 celery sticks, diced
1 tablespoon thyme
2 garlic cloves, crushed
4 tablespoons tomato purée
600 ml (1 pint) hot beef stock
  (see page 98 for homemade)
1 large potato, peeled and cut
  into 1 cm (½ inch) cubes
200 g (7 oz) canned black
  beans, rinsed and drained
200 g (7 oz) canned black-eyed
  beans, rinsed and drained
salt and pepper
lemon wedges, to serve

Serves **4**
Prep time **15 minutes**
Cooking time **30 minutes**

1 Heat the oil in a large heavy-based saucepan, add the beef and fry, stirring, over a medium-high heat for 5-6 minutes until browned.

2 Add the cloves, onion and curry powder and cook for 2-3 minutes until the onions are beginning to soften, then stir in the carrots, celery, thyme, garlic and tomato purée.

3 Pour in the beef stock to just cover the meat and stir well, then add the potato and beans and bring to the boil. Reduce the heat slightly and simmer for 20 minutes, uncovered, or until the potatoes and beef are tender, then season to taste with salt and pepper. Ladle the stew into serving bowls and serve with lemon wedges.

AFFORDABILITY
1

STUDENT TIP

Student kitchens are a favourite hangout for germs, and dirty cloths are germ magnets. If you're unsure of when the dishcloths last had a wash, rinse and squeeze them, then lay out flat in the microwave and zap them for 2–3 minutes.

Rustic Lamb & Potato Curry

1 Heat the oil in a large heavy-based frying pan with a lid and cook the onion and lamb over a high heat, stirring frequently, for 5 minutes, or until the lamb is browned all over and the onion softened.

2 Add the chilli, if using, and cook, stirring, for 1 minute. Stir in the curry paste and cook, stirring, for a further 2 minutes. Add the tomatoes, stock and potatoes and bring to the boil. Reduce the heat, cover and simmer for 10 minutes, then remove the lid and cook for a further 10 minutes, or until the lamb is cooked through and the potatoes are tender.

3 Remove from the heat, then scatter over the coriander and spoon in the yogurt, ready to stir in and serve.

VARIATION

For a simple chicken curry, heat 1 tablespoon vegetable oil in a large heavy-based saucepan and cook 3 thinly sliced boneless, skinless chicken breasts, about 175 g (6 oz) each, over a high heat, stirring, for 3 minutes. Stir in a 400 g (13 oz) jar korma curry sauce and 1 chopped tomato and bring to the boil. Add 200 g (7 oz) baby spinach leaves, then reduce the heat, cover and simmer for 5 minutes, or until the chicken is cooked through. Serve with lightly toasted naan breads.

2 tablespoons vegetable oil

1 large onion, roughly chopped

625 g (1¼ lb) lean lamb, cut into cubes

1 small green chilli, roughly chopped (optional)

4 tablespoons korma curry paste

2 x 400 g (13 oz) cans chopped tomatoes

300 ml (½ pint) chicken stock (see page 11 for homemade)

2 unpeeled potatoes, roughly cut into cubes

50 g (2 oz) fresh coriander, roughly chopped

150 ml (¼ pint) natural yogurt

Serves **4**
Prep time **15 minutes**
Cooking time **30 minutes**

POLLOCK
& Lentils

1 Heat 2 tablespoons of the oil in a flameproof casserole and gently fry the onion for 6–8 minutes until lightly browned. Add the garlic and rosemary, savoury or thyme and cook for about 2 minutes.

2 Stir the lentils into the casserole with the tomatoes, sugar and stock. Bring to a simmer, then cover and cook in a preheated oven, 180°C (350°F), Gas Mark 4, for 10 minutes. Check over the fish for any stray bones and cut into 8 pieces. Season with salt and pepper.

3 Stir the parsley and anchovies into the casserole. Nestle the fish down into the lentils and drizzle the fish with the remaining oil. Re-cover and return to the oven for a further 25 minutes, or until the fish is cooked through. Serve with spoonfuls of garlic mayonnaise.

VARIATION

For a salsa verde sauce, to serve as an alternative accompaniment to the garlic mayonnaise, roughly chop 25 g (1 oz) parsley and 15 g (½ oz) basil and place in a food processor with 1 roughly chopped garlic clove, 15 g (½ oz) pitted green olives, 1 tablespoon rinsed and drained capers in brine and ½ teaspoon Dijon mustard. Process until finely chopped. Add 1 tablespoon lemon juice and 125 ml (4 fl oz) olive oil and process to make a thick sauce. Season to taste with salt and pepper, adding a dash more lemon juice, if liked, for extra tang.

4 tablespoons olive oil
1 onion, finely chopped
4 garlic cloves, crushed
2 teaspoons finely chopped rosemary, savoury or thyme
400 g (13 oz) can green lentils, rinsed and drained
400 g (13 oz) can chopped tomatoes
2 teaspoons caster sugar
150 ml (¼ pint) fish stock (see page 104 for homemade)
625 g (1¼ lb) skinless pollack fillets
4 tablespoons chopped parsley
50 g (2 oz) can anchovy fillets, drained and chopped
salt and pepper
garlic mayonnaise, to serve

Serves **4**
Prep time **15 minutes**
Cooking time **50 minutes**

Mackerel & Sesame NOODLES

1 Put the mackerel in a bowl with the teriyaki sauce and toss to coat the fish with the sauce.

2 Warm the oil in a saucepan, then add the sesame seeds, spring onions, garlic and beans and heat through gently for 2 minutes.

3 Pour in the stock and bring to a gentle simmer. Cover and cook for 5 minutes.

4 Stir the mackerel, noodles, sugar and lime juice into the pan and cook gently for 2 minutes, or until the mackerel is cooked and the broth is hot. Serve immediately.

COOKING TIP
For homemade fish stock, melt 15 g (½ oz) butter in a large saucepan and gently fry 1 kg (2 lb) white fish bones and trimmings until the trimmings have turned opaque. Add a quartered onion, 2 roughly chopped celery sticks, a handful of parsley, several lemon slices and 1 teaspoon peppercorns. Cover with cold water and bring to a gentle simmer. Cook very gently for 30–35 minutes. Strain through a sieve and leave to cool. Cover and chill for up to 2 days or freeze for up to 3 months.

2 large mackerel fillets, about 125 g (4 oz) each, cut into pieces
2 tablespoons teriyaki sauce
2 teaspoons sesame oil
1 tablespoon sesame seeds
½ bunch of spring onions, chopped
1 garlic clove, very thinly sliced
100 g (3½ oz) French beans, topped and tailed and diagonally sliced
400 ml (14 fl oz) fish stock (see tip for homemade)
150 g (5 oz) pack medium straight-to-wok rice noodles
1 teaspoon caster sugar
2 teaspoons lime juice

Serves **2**
Prep time **10 minutes**
Cooking time **12 minutes**

AFFORDABILITY 2

SMOKED HADDOCK
Cannelloni

1. Lightly grease an ovenproof dish with butter. Place the haddock in a bowl, pour over the measured water and leave to stand for 3 minutes. Drain, reserving the water, and break up the fish.

2. Place the watercress in a sieve and pour over boiling water from the kettle until it has wilted. Lay the watercress on a sheet of kitchen paper and squeeze to get rid of excess water. Roughly chop the watercress, then mix it with the haddock and 2 tablespoons of the crème fraîche.

3. Divide the haddock mixture among the lasagne sheets, arranging it in a strip down the middle. Roll up the pasta and arrange snugly, seam-side down, in the prepared ovenproof dish.

4. Mix together the remaining crème fraîche with the haddock soaking water in a mug, season with salt and pepper and pour over the top of the pasta.

5. Scatter the breadcrumbs over the pasta, cover the dish with foil and bake in a preheated oven, 200°C (400°F), Gas Mark 6, for 20 minutes. Remove the foil and cook under a preheated hot grill until the breadcrumbs are golden.

butter, for greasing
400 g (13 oz) skinless smoked haddock fillet, cut into pieces
300 ml (½ pint) boiling water
300 g (10 oz) watercress
200 ml (7 fl oz) crème fraîche
8 fresh lasagne sheets
50 g (2 oz) dried breadcrumbs
salt and pepper

Serves **4**
Prep time **15 minutes, plus standing**
Cooking time **20 minutes**

Spicy TUNA, TOMATO & OLIVE PASTA

AFFORDABILITY
1

350 g (11½ oz) dried penne
2 x 400 g (13 oz) cans tuna
   chunks in water, drained
2 red chillies, finely chopped
1 teaspoon dried red chilli flakes
200 g (7 oz) pitted black olives
240 g (8 oz) tub sun-blush
   tomatoes in oil
salt and pepper
chopped parsley, to garnish

Serves **4**
Prep time **10 minutes**
Cooking time **10 minutes**

1 Cook the pasta in a large saucepan of lightly salted boiling water according to the packet instructions until al dente.

2 Meanwhile, put the tuna in a large bowl and roughly flake with a fork, then add the chillies, chilli flakes, olives and tomatoes with their oil.

3 Drain the pasta, add it to the tuna mixture and toss to mix well, then season with salt and pepper. Spoon into serving bowls, garnish with chopped parsley and serve.

STUDENT TIP

If it has a very long or non-existent use-by date then buy it in bulk. Look out for BOGOF (buy one, get one free) and half-price offers on things like toilet paper, pasta and other dried and canned goods.

BAKED COD
WITH TOMATOES & OLIVES

250 g (8 oz) cherry tomatoes, halved

100 g (3½ oz) pitted black olives

2 tablespoons capers in brine, drained

4 sprigs of thyme, plus extra for garnish

4 cod fillets, about 175 g (6 oz) each

2 tablespoons extra virgin olive oil

2 tablespoons balsamic vinegar

salt and pepper

mixed leaf salad, to serve

Serves **4**
Prep time **5 minutes**
Cooking time **15 minutes**

1 Combine the tomatoes, olives, capers and thyme in a roasting tin. Nestle the cod fillets in the tin, drizzle over the oil and balsamic vinegar and season to taste with salt and pepper. Bake in a preheated oven, 200°C (400°F), Gas Mark 6, for 15 minutes.

2 Transfer the fish, tomatoes and olives to serving plates. Spoon the pan juices over the fish and serve immediately with a mixed leaf salad.

VARIATION
For steamed cod with lemon, arrange a cod fillet on each of 4 x 30 cm (12 inch) squares of foil. Top each with ½ teaspoon grated lemon zest, a squeeze of lemon juice, 1 tablespoon extra virgin olive oil and salt and pepper to taste. Seal the edges of the foil together to form parcels, transfer to a baking sheet and cook in a preheated oven, 200°C (400°F), Gas Mark 6, for 15 minutes. Remove from the oven and leave to rest for 5 minutes. Open the parcels and serve sprinkled with chopped parsley.

PAELLA

1 kg (2 lb) live mussels
4 garlic cloves
1 small bunch of mixed herbs
150 ml (¼ pint) dry white wine
2 litres (3½ pints) hot chicken
   stock (see page 11 for
   homemade) or water
4 tablespoons olive oil
4 small cleaned squid, cut
   into rings
1 large onion, finely chopped
1 red pepper, cored, deseeded
   and chopped
4 large ripe tomatoes, skinned
   (see page 16), deseeded and
   chopped
12 skinless, boneless chicken
   thighs, cut into bite-sized
   pieces
500 g (1 lb) paella rice
large pinch of saffron threads,
   crumbled
125 g (4 oz) fresh or frozen
   peas
12 large raw peeled prawns
salt and pepper

Serves **6**
Prep time **40 minutes**
Cooking time **about 1½ hours**

1 Scrub the mussels in cold water. Scrape off any barnacles and pull away the dark hairy beards. Discard any with damaged shells or open ones that do not close when tapped firmly with a knife. Set aside.

2 Slice 2 of the garlic cloves and crush the remainder. Place the sliced garlic in a large heavy-based saucepan with the herbs, wine and 150 ml (¼ pint) of the stock or water and season well with salt and pepper. Tip in the mussels, cover and cook, shaking the pan frequently, for 4-5 minutes until all the shells have opened. Lift out the mussels with a slotted spoon into a bowl, discarding any that remain closed. Strain the cooking liquid into a bowl and reserve.

3 Heat 2 tablespoons of the oil in the pan and fry the squid, stirring frequently, for 5 minutes. Add the onion, red pepper and crushed garlic and cook gently for 5 minutes, or until softened. Add the mussel cooking liquid and tomatoes and season with salt and pepper. Bring to the boil, then reduce the heat and cook gently, stirring, for 15-20 minutes until thickened. Transfer to a bowl.

4 Heat the remaining oil in the pan, add the chicken and fry for 5 minutes. Add the rice and cook, stirring, for 3 minutes.

5 Return the squid mixture to the pan, add one-third of the remaining stock and the saffron and bring to the boil, stirring. Cover and simmer, adding stock a little at a time, for 30 minutes, or until the chicken is cooked, the rice is tender and the liquid has been absorbed.

6 Taste and adjust the seasoning if needed. Add the peas and prawns and simmer, for 5 minutes, adding a little more stock if required. Return the mussels to the pan, cover and heat through for 5 minutes. Serve immediately.

ROAST SEA BASS
WITH POTATOES
& MUSHROOMS

875 g (1¾ lb) potatoes, peeled
  and cut into 1 cm (½ inch)
  slices
2 garlic cloves, thinly sliced
3 tablespoons olive oil
250 g (8 oz) mixed wild
  mushrooms, sliced if large
4 sea bass fillets, about 175 g
  (6 oz) each
½ tablespoon chopped parsley
salt and pepper
extra virgin olive oil, for
  drizzling

Serves **4**
Prep time **10 minutes**
Cooking time **40-45 minutes**

1 Line a large roasting tin with greaseproof paper. Place the potato slices in the tin, stir in half the garlic and 2 tablespoons of the olive oil and season with salt and pepper. Spread the potatoes out in a single layer, then roast in a preheated oven, 240°C (475°F), Gas Mark 9, for 18-20 minutes until cooked through and golden. Remove from the oven and lift out the potatoes with a slotted spoon on to a plate.

2 Place the tin on the hob, add the remaining oil, the mushrooms and the remaining garlic and cook over high heat, stirring frequently, until the mushrooms are tender. Season with salt and pepper and remove from the heat.

3 Return the roasted potatoes to the tin and stir well. Season the sea bass fillets with salt and pepper, then sit them, skin-side up, on top of the potatoes. Scatter with the parsley and drizzle the fish with the remaining olive oil. Return to the oven and roast for 10-12 minutes until the fish is cooked through. Serve immediately with a drizzle of extra virgin olive oil.

AFFORDABILITY
3

Spicy PRAWN & PEA PILAU

1. Heat the oil and butter in a heavy-based saucepan, add the onion and cook over a medium heat for 2-3 minutes until softened. Stir in the garlic and curry paste and cook for a further 1-2 minutes until fragrant, then add the rice and stir to coat well.

2. Stir in the stock, peas and lime zest, then season well with salt and pepper and bring to the boil. Cover tightly, then reduce the heat to low and cook for 12-15 minutes until the liquid is absorbed and the rice is tender.

3. Remove from the heat, then stir in the lime juice, coriander and prawns. Cover and leave to stand for a few minutes to allow the prawns to heat through before serving.

VARIATION

For spicy prawn and pea stir-fried rice, heat 2 tablespoons sunflower oil in a large wok or frying pan until hot, add 1 tablespoon medium curry paste, 400 g (13 oz) ready-cooked peeled prawns, 200 g (7 oz) frozen peas and 500 g (1 lb) ready-cooked basmati rice and stir-fry over a high heat for 4-5 minutes until piping hot. Remove from the heat, season with salt and pepper and stir in 6 tablespoons chopped fresh coriander. Serve immediately.

1 tablespoon sunflower oil
1 tablespoon butter
1 large onion, finely chopped
2 garlic cloves, finely chopped
1 tablespoon medium or hot curry paste
250 g (8 oz) basmati rice
600 ml (1 pint) hot fish or vegetable stock (see pages 104 or 15 for homemade)
300 g (10 oz) frozen peas
finely grated zest and juice of 1 large lime
20 g (¾ oz) fresh coriander, finely chopped
400 g (13 oz) ready-cooked peeled prawns
salt and pepper

Serves **4**
Prep time **10 minutes, plus standing**
Cooking time **20-25 minutes**

AFFORDABILITY 2

GOATS' CHEESE & PEPPER *Lasagne*

325 g (11 oz) can or jar
  pimientos, drained and
  roughly chopped
6 tomatoes, skinned (see page
  16) and roughly chopped
1 yellow pepper, cored,
  deseeded and finely chopped
2 courgettes, thinly sliced
75 g (3 oz) sun-dried tomatoes,
  thinly sliced
100 g (3½ oz) sun-dried tomato
  pesto
25 g (1 oz) basil
4 tablespoons olive oil
150 g (5 oz) soft goats' cheese,
  crumbled
600 ml (1 pint) ready-made
  cheese sauce (see tip for
  homemade)
150 g (5 oz) dried egg lasagne
6 tablespoons grated Parmesan
  cheese
salt and pepper
mixed leaf salad, to serve

Serves **4**
Prep time **20 minutes, plus
    standing**
Cooking time **50 minutes-1 hour**

1 Place the pimientos in a bowl with the tomatoes, yellow pepper, courgettes, tomatoes and pesto. Tear the basil leaves and add to the bowl with the oil and a little salt and pepper. Mix together thoroughly.

2 Spoon a quarter of the tomato mixture into a 1.8 litre (3 pint) shallow ovenproof dish and dot with a quarter of the goats' cheese and 4 tablespoons of the cheese sauce. Cover with a third of the lasagne sheets in a layer, breaking them to fit where necessary. Repeat the layering, finishing with a layer of the tomato mixture and goats' cheese.

3 Spoon over the remaining cheese sauce and sprinkle with the Parmesan. Bake in a preheated oven, 190°C (375°F), Gas Mark 5, for 50 minutes-1 hour until deep golden. Leave to stand for 10 minutes before serving with a mixed leaf salad.

COOKING TIP
For a homemade cheese sauce, place 500 ml (17 fl oz) milk in a saucepan with 1 small onion and 1 bay leaf. Heat until just boiling, then remove from the heat and leave to infuse for 20 minutes. Strain the milk into a jug. Melt 50 g (2 oz) butter in the cleaned saucepan, add 50 g (2 oz) plain flour and stir in quickly. Cook over a medium heat, stirring, for 1-2 minutes, then remove from the heat and gradually whisk in the infused milk until blended. Return to the heat, bring gently to the boil, stirring, and cook for 2 minutes until the sauce has thickened. Remove from the heat and stir in 125 g (4 oz) grated Cheddar or Gruyère cheese until melted.

Veggie
BEAN CHILLI

1. Heat the oil in a large flameproof casserole dish. Add the onion and cook for 5 minutes until softened, then add the red pepper, garlic, spices and herbs and cook for 30 seconds. Pour in the tomatoes and season to taste with salt and pepper. Bring to the boil, then reduce the heat and simmer for 10 minutes.

2. Add the beans and sweetcorn to the pan and cook for a further 3-4 minutes until heated through. Divide among serving bowls and top each portion with a spoonful of soured cream. Sprinkle with the chopped coriander and grated cheese and serve with tortilla chips.

2 tablespoons vegetable oil
1 onion, finely chopped
1 red pepper, cored, deseeded and sliced
1 garlic clove, crushed
1 teaspoon ground cumin
1 teaspoon chipotle paste or a pinch of chilli powder
1 teaspoon dried oregano
½ teaspoon ground coriander
400 g (13 oz) can chopped tomatoes
400 g (13 oz) can black beans, rinsed and drained
150 g (5 oz) canned sweetcorn, drained

To serve
soured cream
handful of chopped fresh coriander
grated Cheddar cheese
salt and pepper
tortilla chips

Serves **4**
Prep time **10 minutes**
Cooking time **20 minutes**

Middle Eastern
COURGETTE, TOMATO
& MINT CURRY

 Vegan

2 tablespoons olive oil
2 onions, finely sliced
4 courgettes, cut into 1 cm
   (½ inch) cubes
2 x 400 g (13 oz) cans peeled
   plum tomatoes
2 garlic cloves, crushed
1 teaspoon mild chilli powder
¼ teaspoon ground turmeric
2 teaspoons dried mint
salt and pepper
small handful of finely chopped
   mint, to garnish

Serves **4**
Prep time **10 minutes**
Cooking time **25-30 minutes**

1 Heat the oil in a large heavy-based saucepan, add the onions and cook over a medium-low heat, stirring occasionally, for 6-8 minutes until softened. Add the courgettes and cook, stirring occasionally, for a further 5-6 minutes until tender.

2 Increase the heat to medium, add the tomatoes and garlic and cook for 10-12 minutes until the sauce is thickened. Stir in the chilli powder, turmeric and dried mint and cook for a further 2-3 minutes. Season well with salt and pepper. Ladle the curry into serving bowls and garnish with the chopped mint.

AFFORDABILITY
1

SPICY GREEN BEAN, POTATO & PESTO LINGUINI

1 Cook the potatoes in a large saucepan of lightly salted boiling water for 10-12 minutes until just tender, adding the beans and linguine 4 minutes before the end of the cooking time. Drain well, then return to the pan.

2 Mix together the chillies and pesto in a mug, then season well with salt and pepper. Spoon into the pasta mixture and toss to mix well. Divide among serving bowls and serve with grated pecorino cheese to sprinkle over.

200 g (7 oz) potatoes, peeled and cut into small cubes
200 g (7 oz) green beans, trimmed and halved
350 g (11½ oz) fresh linguine
2 red chillies, finely chopped
250 g (8 oz) shop-bought fresh green pesto
salt and pepper
grated pecorino cheese, to serve

Serves **4**
Prep time **10 minutes**
Cooking time **15 minutes**

AFFORDABILITY
2

Creamy Chilli & COURGETTES

1. Heat the oil and butter in a large frying pan. Add the chillies, garlic, spring onions and courgettes and cook over a medium-low heat for 10 minutes, or until softened.

2. Reduce the heat to low, add the lime zest and gently cook for 3–4 minutes, then add the cream cheese and mix together until the cheese melts. Season to taste with salt and pepper, stir in the parsley and serve with cooked pasta.

1 tablespoon olive oil
1 tablespoon butter
2 red chillies, finely chopped
2 garlic cloves, finely chopped
4 spring onions, very finely chopped
3 courgettes, coarsely grated
finely grated zest of 1 lime
150 g (5 oz) cream cheese
small handful of parsley, chopped
salt and pepper
cooked pasta, such as pennette or other short-shaped pasta, to serve

Serves **4**
Prep time **15 minutes**
Cooking time **15 minutes**

STUDENT TIP

Price comparison websites help you quickly locate the cheapest prices for your groceries. Forget about brand loyalty — follow the bargains to stretch your budget. Some supermarkets also now run a price-check on every shop and will apply the discount (if applicable) on your next visit.

Green veg CURRY

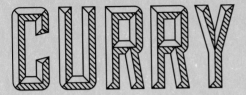

 Vegan

AFFORDABILITY 1

1 tablespoon sunflower oil

3 tablespoons Thai green curry paste (see page 132 for homemade)

2 red chillies, deseeded and finely sliced (optional)

400 ml (14 fl oz) can coconut milk

200 ml (7 fl oz) vegetable stock (see page 15 for homemade)

6 kaffir lime leaves or 1 tablespoon finely grated lime zest

2 tablespoons soy sauce

1 tablespoon soft brown sugar

200 g (7 oz) carrots, cut into thick batons

250 g (8 oz) butternut squash, peeled, deseeded and cut into 1.5 cm (¾ inch) cubes

100 g (3½ oz) sugar snap peas

10 tablespoons finely chopped fresh coriander

juice of 1 lime

steamed jasmine rice, to serve

Serves **4**
Prep time **15 minutes**
Cooking time **15-20 minutes**

1 Heat the oil in a large nonstick saucepan. Add the curry paste and chillies, if using, and stir-fry for 2-3 minutes.

2 Stir in the coconut milk, stock, lime leaves or lime zest, soy sauce, sugar, carrots and butternut squash. Simmer, uncovered for 6-8 minutes, stirring occasionally. Add the sugar snap peas and continue to simmer for 4-5 minutes.

3 Remove from the heat and stir in the coriander and lime juice. Ladle the curry into serving bowls and serve with steamed jasmine rice.

PESTO PUFF TART

375 g (12 oz) pack ready-rolled
  puff pastry
3 tablespoons shop-bought
  fresh green pesto
300 g (10 oz) yellow and red
  cherry tomatoes, halved
150 g (5 oz) mixed antipasti
  (artichokes, roasted peppers,
  mushrooms and aubergines),
  from a jar, drained
100 g (3½ oz) goats' cheese,
  crumbled
basil leaves, to garnish

Serves **4**
Prep time **10 minutes**
Cooking time **15-20 minutes**

1 Lay the puff pastry on a baking sheet. Score a 2.5 cm (1 inch) margin around the edge and prick the base with a fork.

2 Top with the pesto, tomatoes, mixed antipasti and goats' cheese. Bake in a preheated oven, 200°C (400°F), Gas Mark 6, for 15-20 minutes. Garnish with the basil leaves and serve.

AFFORDABILITY
2

Ranch-style EGGS (V)

2 tablespoons olive oil
1 onion, finely sliced
1 red chilli, deseeded and finely chopped
1 garlic clove, crushed
1 teaspoon ground cumin
1 teaspoon dried oregano
400 g (13 oz) canned cherry tomatoes
200 g (7 oz) roasted red and yellow peppers in oil (from a jar), drained and roughly chopped
4 eggs
salt and pepper
4 tablespoons finely chopped fresh coriander, to garnish

Serves **4**
Prep time **10 minutes**
Cooking time **15 minutes**

1 Heat the oil in a large frying pan with a lid. Add the onion, chilli, garlic, cumin and oregano and fry gently for 5 minutes, or until softened.

2 Stir in the tomatoes and red and yellow peppers and cook for a further 5 minutes, adding a splash of water if the sauce looks dry. Season well with salt and pepper.

3 Make 4 hollows in the sauce and break an egg into each hollow. Cover and cook for 5 minutes, or until the eggs are just set. Serve immediately, garnished with the chopped coriander.

VARIATION

For a Mexican-style sauce, heat 2 tablespoons olive oil in a large frying pan and add 1 finely chopped onion, 1 finely chopped red chilli, 1 teaspoon each of ground cumin and dried oregano, 2 x 400 g (13 oz) cans cherry tomatoes and 200 g (7 oz) chopped roasted red peppers in oil (from a jar, drained). Season with salt and pepper, bring to the boil and cook over a medium heat for 12–15 minutes. Stir in a small handful of chopped coriander and serve over cooked pasta or rice.

OH SO QUICK & EASY

BALSAMIC ROAST TOMATOES

CHICKEN BREASTS WITH
MASCARPONE & TOMATOES

THAI GREEN PORK CURRY

BOSTON BAKED BEANS

Sticky
LEMON CHICKEN
NOODLES

2 tablespoons vegetable oil
300 g (10 oz) chicken fillets,
 cut into thin strips
200 g (7 oz) Tenderstem
 broccoli
2 garlic cloves, crushed
2 teaspoons finely grated fresh
 root ginger
1 red chilli, finely chopped
finely grated zest and juice
 of 1 lemon
1 tablespoon clear honey
2 teaspoons light soy sauce
300 g (10 oz) ready-cooked egg
 noodles
handful of roasted cashew nuts,
 to garnish

Serves **4**
Prep time **10 minutes**
Cooking time **10 minutes**

1 Heat a large wok until smoking hot. Add the oil and
swirl around the pan, then add the chicken and cook
for 1 minute. Add the broccoli and cook for a further
5 minutes, or until the chicken is nearly cooked through.
Add the garlic, ginger and chilli to the wok and cook for
1 minute more. Then add the lemon zest and juice,
honey and soy sauce and toss around the pan.

2 Add the noodles and a splash of water and cook until
heated through. Divide among serving bowls, garnish
with the cashew nuts and serve.

CHICKEN BREASTS
WITH MASCARPONE & TOMATOES

4 tablespoons mascarpone
cheese
4 teaspoons shop-bought fresh
green pesto
4 skinless chicken breast fillets
100 g (3½ oz) dried
breadcrumbs
3 tablespoons olive oil, plus
extra for greasing
150 g (5 oz) cherry tomatoes
25 g (1 oz) toasted pine nuts
salt and pepper
crusty bread, to serve (optional)

Serves **4**
Prep time **10 minutes**
Cooking time **15 minutes**

1 Mix together the mascarpone and pesto in a bowl. Cut a
horizontal slit in the side of each chicken breast to form
a pocket. Fill the pockets with the mascarpone mixture.

2 Spread out the breadcrumbs on a plate. Season the
chicken breasts with salt and pepper, rub them with
1 tablespoon of the oil and then roll them in the
breadcrumbs until well coated.

3 Place the chicken breasts in a roasting tin, drizzle over
another tablespoon of the oil and bake in a preheated
oven, 200°C (400°F), Gas Mark 6, for 10 minutes.

4 Add the tomatoes to the tin, season with salt and pepper
and drizzle with the remaining oil. Return to the oven for
a further 5 minutes, or until the chicken is cooked
through. Scatter over the pine nuts and serve with
crusty bread, if liked.

AFFORDABILITY 3

Chicken drumstick
JAMBALAYA

1. Heat the oil in a large saucepan. Cut a few slashes across the thickest part of the drumsticks, add them to the pan and fry over a high heat for 5 minutes, turning occasionally. Add the onion, garlic, celery, chilli and green pepper and cook for a further 2-3 minutes until softened.

2. Add the chorizo, fry briefly, then add the rice, stirring to coat the grains in the pan juices. Pour in the stock, add the bay leaf and bring to the boil. Cover, reduce the heat and simmer for 20 minutes, stirring occasionally, until the stock has been absorbed and the rice is tender.

3. Stir in the tomatoes and Tabasco sauce and season to taste with salt and pepper. Heat through for 3 minutes before serving.

1 tablespoon sunflower oil
8 skinless chicken drumsticks
1 onion, chopped
2 garlic cloves, crushed
2 celery sticks, sliced
1 red chilli, deseeded and chopped
1 green pepper, cored, deseeded and chopped
75 g (3 oz) chorizo sausage, sliced
250 ml (8 fl oz) long-grain rice
500 ml (17 fl oz) chicken stock (see page 11 for homemade)
1 bay leaf
3 tomatoes, cut into wedges
dash of Tabasco sauce
salt and pepper

Serves **4**
Prep time **15 minutes**
Cooking time **30 minutes**

AFFORDABILITY
2

French-style
CHICKEN STEW

1 Place the leek, chicken, potatoes and carrot in a large saucepan. Pour in the stock and wine and season to taste with salt and pepper. Bring to the boil, then reduce the heat and simmer for 15 minutes, or until the chicken and vegetables are just cooked through.

2 Stir in the peas and crème fraîche and heat through. Scatter over the chopped tarragon and serve immediately.

1 leek, trimmed, cleaned and sliced
4 boneless, skinless chicken thighs, cut into chunks
400 g (13 oz) small new potatoes, halved
1 carrot, sliced
400 ml (14 fl oz) hot chicken stock (see page 11 for homemade)
50 ml (2 fl oz) dry white wine
100 g (3½ oz) frozen peas, defrosted
2 tablespoons crème fraîche
salt and pepper
handful of chopped tarragon, to garnish

Serves **4**
Prep time **10 minutes**
Cooking time **20 minutes**

AFFORDABILITY
2

CHICKEN & SPINACH Stew

AFFORDABILITY
2

625 g (1¼ lb) skinless, boneless chicken thighs, thinly sliced
2 teaspoons ground cumin
1 teaspoon ground ginger
2 tablespoons olive oil
1 tablespoon tomato purée
2 x 400 g (13 oz) cans cherry tomatoes
50 g (2 oz) raisins
250 g (8 oz) ready-cooked Puy lentils
1 teaspoon grated lemon zest
150 g (5 oz) baby spinach leaves
salt and pepper
handful of chopped parsley, to garnish
steamed couscous or rice, to serve

Serves **4**
Prep time **10 minutes**
Cooking time **20 minutes**

1 Mix the chicken with the cumin and ginger in a bowl until well coated. Heat the oil in a large saucepan, then add the chicken and cook for 2–3 minutes until lightly browned.

2 Stir in the tomato purée, tomatoes, raisins, lentils and lemon zest, season with salt and pepper and simmer gently for about 12 minutes until thickened slightly and the chicken is cooked.

3 Add the spinach and stir until wilted. Ladle the stew into bowls, then garnish with the chopped parsley and serve with steamed couscous or rice.

Chicken & BEANS

1 tablespoon olive oil
2 boneless, skinless chicken
  breasts, each about 150 g
  (5 oz), thinly sliced
1 onion, thinly sliced
1 tablespoon black treacle
1 tablespoon wholegrain
  mustard
1 tablespoon soft dark brown
  sugar
400 g (13 oz) can chopped
  tomatoes
400 g (13 oz) can baked beans
3 tablespoons chopped parsley
pepper
4 thick slices of wholemeal
  toast, to serve

....
Serves **4**
Prep time **5 minutes**
Cooking time **10 minutes**
....

1 Heat the oil in a heavy-based saucepan and cook the chicken and onion over a medium heat for 3-4 minutes.

2 Add the treacle, mustard, sugar and tomatoes, bring to the boil and simmer for 2 minutes. Stir in the beans and parsley and cook for a further 1 minute, or until heated through.

3 Spoon the mixture on to the slices of wholemeal toast, season with pepper and serve immediately.

PORK & TOMATO RICE POT

1 Heat 1 tablespoon of the oil in a large, deep frying pan with a lid. Add the pork fillet and cook over a high heat for 3 minutes, or until golden and nearly cooked through. Lift out with a slotted spoon on to a plate.

2 Reduce the heat, add the remaining oil and the onion to the pan and cook for 3 minutes, or until softened. Stir in the garlic and cook for 30 seconds, then stir in the rice and cook for 1 minute. Add the paprika and tomatoes, bring to the boil and simmer for 2-3 minutes.

3 Pour in the stock, season to taste with salt and pepper and cook for 12-15 minutes until there is just a little liquid left around the edges of the pan.

4 Lightly fork the spinach through the rice, arrange the pork on top, then cover and cook for a further 3-4 minutes until the pork is cooked through. Serve with lemon wedges.

3 tablespoons olive oil
300 g (10 oz) pork fillet, sliced
1 onion, finely chopped
3 garlic cloves, finely chopped
250 g (8 oz) paella rice
2 teaspoons smoked paprika
200 g (7 oz) can chopped
  tomatoes
650 ml (1 pint 2 fl oz) hot
  chicken stock (see page 11 for
  homemade)
125 g (4 oz) baby spinach
  leaves
salt and pepper
lemon wedges, to serve

Serves **4**
Prep time **10 minutes**
Cooking time **25-30 minutes**

AFFORDABILITY
2

THAI GREEN
PORK CURRY

2 tablespoons olive oil
4 boneless pork steaks, cut into bite-sized pieces
2 tablespoons Thai green curry paste (see tip for homemade)
400 ml (14 fl oz) can coconut milk
100 g (3½ oz) green beans
200 g (7 oz) can water chestnuts, drained, rinsed and cut in half
juice of 1 lime, or to taste
1 handful of fresh coriander leaves
boiled rice, to serve

Serves **4**
Prep time **10 minutes**
Cooking time **20 minutes**

1 Heat the oil in a large saucepan, add the pork and cook, stirring, for 3-4 minutes until browned all over. Add the curry paste and cook, stirring, for 1 minute until fragrant.

2 Pour in the coconut milk, stir and reduce the heat to a gentle simmer. Cook for 10 minutes, then add the beans and water chestnuts and cook for a further 3 minutes.

3 Remove from the heat, add lime juice to taste and stir through the coriander. Serve immediately with boiled rice.

COOKING TIP
For homemade Thai green curry paste, put 15 small green chillies, 4 halved garlic cloves, 2 finely chopped lemon grass stalks, 2 torn lime leaves, 2 chopped shallots, 50 g (2 oz) fresh coriander leaves, stalks and roots, 2.5 cm (1 inch) piece of fresh root ginger, peeled and finely chopped, 2 teaspoons black peppercorns, 1 teaspoon pared lime zest, ½ teaspoon salt and 1 tablespoon groundnut oil into a food processor or blender and process to a thick paste. Alternatively, use a pestle and mortar to crush the ingredients, working in the oil at the end. Transfer the paste to an airtight container; it can be stored in a refrigerator for up to 3 weeks.

AFFORDABILITY
2

Pork & RED PEPPER CHILLI

2 tablespoons olive oil
1 large onion, chopped
2 garlic cloves, crushed
1 red pepper, cored, deseeded
and diced
450 g (14½ oz) minced pork
1 red chilli, finely chopped
1 teaspoon dried oregano
500 g (1 lb) passata
400 g (13 oz) can red kidney
beans, rinsed and drained
salt and pepper

To serve
soured cream
boiled rice or crusty bread

Serves **4**
Prep time **10 minutes**
Cooking time **30 minutes**

1 Heat the oil in a saucepan, add the onion, garlic and red pepper and cook for 5 minutes, or until softened and starting to brown. Add the pork and cook, stirring and breaking up the mince with a wooden spoon, for 5 minutes, or until browned.

2 Add all the remaining ingredients to the pan and bring to the boil. Reduce the heat and simmer gently for 20 minutes. Remove from the heat and season well with salt and pepper. Divide among serving bowls, top with a dollop of soured cream and serve with boiled rice or crusty bread.

VARIATION
For a lamb and aubergine chilli, substitute the pork mince and red pepper with 1 aubergine and 450 g (14½ oz) lamb mince. Cut the aubergine into small cubes and fry as above with the lamb mince. Garnish the finished dish with 2 tablespoons of finely chopped mint leaves and serve with boiled rice or pasta.

AFFORDABILITY
1

BEEF STEW *with* GARLIC BREAD TOPPING

1 Heat 1 tablespoon of the oil in a flameproof casserole over a high heat. Add the beef and cook for 2-3 minutes until golden. Lift out with a slotted spoon on to a plate.

2 Add the remaining oil to the casserole together with the onion, carrot and celery and cook for 5 minutes, or until softened. Stir in the tomato purée, flour and thyme, then pour in the wine and cook for 2-3 minutes until reduced by half. Pour in the stock and simmer for 15 minutes.

3 Return the meat to the casserole, season with salt and pepper and mix well. Arrange the garlic bread slices on top of the stew. Cook under a preheated hot grill for 3 minutes, or until the bread is golden and crisp.

2 tablespoons olive oil
400 g (13 oz) beef steak,
    cut into chunks
1 onion, sliced
1 carrot, sliced
1 celery stick, sliced
1 teaspoon tomato purée
2 teaspoons plain flour
handful of chopped thyme
100 ml (3½ fl oz) red wine
200 ml (7 fl oz) hot beef stock
    (see page 98 for homemade)
½ ready-made garlic bread
    baguette, sliced
salt and pepper

Serves **4**
Prep time **10 minutes**
Cooking time **30 minutes**

AFFORDABILITY
2

Creamy coconut
BEEF RENDANG

2 tablespoons vegetable oil
1 tablespoon peeled and finely
   chopped fresh root ginger
1 bird's eye chilli, thinly sliced
1 garlic clove, thinly sliced
1 lemon grass stalk, thinly
   sliced
500 g (1 lb) frying steak, cut
   into strips
½ teaspoon ground cinnamon
pinch of ground turmeric
juice of 1 lime
400 g (13 oz) can coconut milk
4 tablespoons chopped fresh
   coriander
steamed Thai jasmine rice,
   to serve (optional)

Serves **4**
Prep time **10 minutes**
Cooking time **10 minutes**

1 Heat the oil in a large, heavy-based frying pan or wok
and cook the ginger, chilli, garlic and lemon grass over
a medium heat, stirring frequently, for 1–2 minutes until
softened but not coloured. Add the beef, increase the
heat to high and stir-fry for 5 minutes, or until browned
and cooked through.

2 Stir in the cinnamon and turmeric and cook, stirring, for
a few seconds before adding the lime juice and coconut
milk. Gently heat, stirring, for 2–3 minutes until the sauce
is hot. Serve immediately with the steamed jasmine rice,
if liked, and scatter with the chopped coriander.

VARIATION

For speedy Thai-style beef and coconut skewers, cut 500 g
(1 lb) fillet steak into chunks. Thread the steak on to 8 metal
skewers alternately with 2 red peppers, cored, deseeded and
cut into chunky pieces. Mix 4 tablespoons Thai red curry
paste with 200 ml (7 fl oz)
coconut cream in a bowl
and spoon over the
skewers. Cook the beef
skewers under a
preheated hot grill for
3–4 minutes on each side
until cooked through.
Serve with warm pitta
bread.

PEA & LAMB KORMA

2 tablespoons olive oil
1 onion, chopped
2 garlic cloves, crushed
250 g (8 oz) potatoes, cut into
  1.5 cm (¾ inch) dice
500 g (1 lb) minced lamb
1 tablespoon korma curry
  powder
200 g (7 oz) frozen peas
200 ml (7 fl oz) vegetable stock
  (see page 15 for homemade)
2 tablespoons mango chutney
salt and pepper
chopped fresh coriander,
  to garnish

To serve
natural yogurt
steamed rice

Serves **4**
Prep time **10 minutes**
Cooking time **30 minutes**

1 Heat the oil in a saucepan, add the onion and garlic and cook for 5 minutes, or until the onion is soft and starting to brown. Add the potatoes and lamb and cook, stirring and breaking up the mince with a wooden spoon, for 5 minutes, or until the meat has browned.

2 Add the curry powder and cook, stirring, for 1 minute. Add the remaining ingredients and season to taste with salt and pepper. Bring to the boil, then reduce the heat, cover tightly and simmer for 20 minutes. Divide among serving bowls, garnish with the chopped coriander and serve with natural yogurt and steamed rice.

STUDENT TIP

Buy rice, spices and other ethnic ingredients from specialist shops — you'll find it's much cheaper than buying in the supermarket. If you make a lot of curries and tagines, larger jars of spices will be a lot more economical, and you can buy super-size sacks of rice and pulses that will keep your cupboards stocked for weeks.

Crispy FISH PIE

butter, for greasing
200 g (7 oz) frozen spinach
400 g (13 oz) skinless salmon
   fillet, cubed
250 g (8 oz) skinless smoked
   haddock fillet, cubed
4 eggs
100 ml (3½ fl oz) crème fraîche
2 tablespoons boiling water
50 g (2 oz) dried breadcrumbs
salt and pepper

Serves **4**
Prep time **15 minutes**
Cooking time **25 minutes**

1 Lightly grease an ovenproof dish with butter. Place the spinach in a sieve and pour over boiling water from the kettle until it has defrosted. Lay the spinach on a sheet of kitchen paper and squeeze to get rid of excess water.

2 Arrange the spinach in the prepared ovenproof dish and place the fish on top. Make 4 small hollows between the fish pieces and crack an egg into each one.

3 Mix the crème fraîche with the measured water in a mug, season to taste with salt and pepper and pour over the fish.

4 Sprinkle the breadcrumbs over the top of the pie. Place in a preheated oven, 200°C (400°F), Gas Mark 6, for 25 minutes, or until golden and bubbling and the fish is cooked through.

VARIATION
For crispy fish nuggets, cut 400 g (13 oz) chunky skinless salmon fillet into small bite-sized pieces. Toss the salmon with 3 tablespoons olive oil in a bowl. Place 100 g (3½ oz) dried white breadcrumbs, the finely grated zest of 1 lemon, a handful of chopped parsley and a pinch of salt in a freezer bag. Add the salmon and shake until well coated, then arrange the salmon on a lightly greased baking sheet. Drizzle with another tablespoon of olive oil, then cook under a preheated hot grill for 5 minutes. Turn over and cook for a further 2-3 minutes until golden and cooked through. Serve with a tomato salad.

FARFALLE WITH TUNA SAUCE

125 g (4 oz) can tuna in olive oil, drained
2 tablespoons extra virgin olive oil, plus extra to taste (optional)
4 tomatoes, roughly chopped
50 g (2 oz) pitted black olives, roughly chopped
grated zest of 1 lemon
2 garlic cloves, crushed
2 tablespoons roughly chopped parsley
350 g (11½ oz) dried farfalle
salt

Serves **4**
Prep time **10 minutes, plus standing**
Cooking time **10 minutes**

1 Put the tuna in a large bowl and break it up with a fork. Stir in the oil, tomatoes, olives, lemon zest, garlic and parsley and season with salt. Cover and leave to stand for at least 30 minutes (including the pasta's cooking time).

2 Meanwhile, cook the pasta in a large saucepan of salted boiling water according to the packet instructions until al dente. Drain well, then add to the bowl with the tuna sauce and toss to combine. Serve immediately with a drizzle of extra virgin olive oil, if liked.

COOKING TIP
To serve this dish as a pasta salad, refresh the cooked pasta in cold running water before adding the remaining ingredients.

Steamed
LEMON
SALMON &
POTATOES

1. Set a large steamer over a saucepan of gently simmering water. Place the potatoes in the steamer and season well with salt and pepper. Cover and cook for 10 minutes.

2. Place the salmon on top of the potatoes and scatter around the beans. Cover and cook for a further 7-10 minutes until the fish and vegetables are cooked through.

3. Meanwhile, mix together the crème fraîche, lemon zest and juice, dill and capers in a mug and season to taste with salt and pepper. Serve the salmon and vegetables with the crème fraîche mixture.

400 g (13 oz) new potatoes, sliced
2 salmon fillets
75 g (3 oz) French beans, topped and tailed
4 tablespoons crème fraîche
finely grated zest and juice of ½ lemon
handful of chopped dill
1 tablespoon capers, rinsed and drained
salt and pepper

Serves **2**
Prep time **10 minutes**
Cooking time **20 minutes**

AFFORDABILITY
2

Smoked Haddock KEDGEREE

1 tablespoon vegetable oil
25 g (1 oz) butter
1 onion, finely chopped
1 garlic clove, crushed
1 teaspoon finely grated fresh
  root ginger
1 teaspoon cumin seeds
½ teaspoon coriander seeds
1 teaspoon curry powder
½ teaspoon ground turmeric
300 g (10 oz) basmati rice
650 ml (1 pint 2 fl oz) hot
  chicken or fish stock (see
  pages 11 or 104 for
  homemade)
300 g (10 oz) skinless smoked
  haddock fillet
75 g (3 oz) frozen peas
1 red chilli, chopped
handful of chopped fresh
  coriander
salt and pepper
mango chutney, to serve

....

Serves **4**
Prep time **10 minutes**
Cooking time **25 minutes**

....

1 Heat the oil and butter in a large saucepan. Add the onion and cook for 5 minutes, then stir in the garlic and ginger and cook for 1 minute. Add the cumin and coriander seeds and cook for 30 seconds, then stir in the curry powder, turmeric and rice and cook for a further 1 minute.

2 Pour in the stock and cook for 5 minutes. Place the fish on top of the rice and cook for a further 5 minutes. By this time, most of the stock should have boiled away.

3 Add the peas, cover the pan tightly with a lid, turn down the heat as low as it will go and cook for 5–7 minutes until the rice is cooked through.

4 Use a fork to gently break up the fish, stir the fish and peas into the rice and season to taste with salt and pepper. Scatter with the chilli and coriander and serve with mango chutney.

AFFORDABILITY 2

BAKED COD PARCELS
WITH BEANS & CHORIZO

4 cod fillets
400 g (13 oz) can butter beans,
    rinsed and drained
125 g (4 oz) cherry tomatoes,
    halved
4 sprigs of thyme
4 thin slices of chorizo sausage
75 ml (3 fl oz) dry white wine
salt and pepper

Serves **4**
Prep time **10 minutes**
Cooking time **15 minutes**

1 Cut 4 large sheets of baking paper and place a cod fillet on each. Divide the beans, tomatoes and thyme among the cod fillets.

2 Place a chorizo slice on top of each piece of fish and season well with salt and pepper, then fold the paper over and roll up the edges to create airtight parcels, leaving just a little gap.

3 Pour a little wine into each parcel and then fully seal, leaving enough space in the packages for air to circulate. Place on a baking sheet and bake in a preheated oven, 220°C (425°F), Gas Mark 7, for 15 minutes, or until the fish is cooked through.

VARIATION
For seared cod with bean and tomato salad, rub 1 tablespoon olive oil over 4 cod fillets and season well with salt and pepper. Place the cod, skin-side down, in a preheated griddle and cook for 5 minutes. Turn over and cook for a further 3 minutes, or until golden and cooked through. Meanwhile, make a dressing by whisking together 1 tablespoon balsamic vinegar and 3 tablespoons olive oil in a bowl. Toss the dressing with 250 g (8 oz) halved cherry tomatoes and a 400 g (13 oz) can butter beans, rinsed and drained, 100 g (3½ oz) rocket and ½ chopped red chilli and season to taste with salt and pepper. Serve the salad with the cod.

AFFORDABILITY
3

OVEN-BAKED FISH & CHIPS
WITH TOMATO SALSA

1   Place the potatoes in a roasting tin. Drizzle over half
    the oil, season well with salt and pepper and toss
    to make sure the potatoes are coated in oil. Bake
    in a preheated oven, 220°C (425°F), Gas Mark 7, for
    10 minutes.

2   Turn over the potatoes, place the fish on top, season
    again and scatter over the lemon zest. Return to the
    oven for a further 15-20 minutes until the potatoes
    are just cooked through.

3   Meanwhile, make the tomato salsa. Mix together the
    remaining oil and the vinegar in a bowl and season
    to taste with salt and pepper. Stir in the tomatoes,
    capers and spring onion.

4   Transfer the fish to serving plates, garnish with the
    chopped parsley and serve with the chips and salsa
    on the side.

VARIATION

For fish fingers with sweet potato chips, toss 750 g
(1½ lb) sweet potatoes, peeled and cut into thin
wedges, with 2 tablespoons olive oil in a roasting
tin. Season to taste with salt and pepper, then bake
in a preheated oven, 200°C (400°F), Gas Mark 6,
for 7 minutes. Meanwhile, brush 3 tablespoons
mayonnaise over 400 g (13 oz) skinless cod fillet,
cut into fingers. Finely grate the zest of 1 lemon
and mix with 75 g (3 oz) dried breadcrumbs on
a plate. Toss the fish in the crumbs until coated.
Place in the roasting tin and return to the oven
for a further 10 minutes, or until cooked through.

750 g (1½ lb) potatoes, cut into
   thin wedges
4 tablespoons olive oil
4 skinless cod or haddock fillets
finely grated zest of 1 lemon
1 teaspoon balsamic vinegar
4 tomatoes, chopped
1 teaspoon capers, rinsed and
   drained
1 spring onion, chopped
salt and pepper
handful of chopped parsley,
   to garnish

Serves **4**
Prep time **10 minutes**
Cooking time **25-30 minutes**

Mixed Seafood
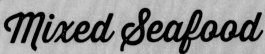
CASSEROLE

4 tablespoons olive oil
1 onion, diced
4 garlic cloves, crushed
100 ml (3½ fl oz) white wine
400 g (13 oz) can chopped
  tomatoes
200 ml (7 fl oz) fish stock (see
  page 104 for homemade)
pinch of saffron threads
400 g (13 oz) pack ready-
  cooked mixed seafood
2 tablespoons chopped parsley
crusty bread, to serve
  (optional)

Serves **4**
Prep time **5 minutes**
Cooking time **15 minutes**

1 Heat the oil in a heavy-based saucepan and sauté the onion and garlic for 3-4 minutes. Pour in the wine and boil for 2-3 minutes, then add the tomatoes, stock and saffron. Bring to a simmer, stir in the mixed seafood and parsley and cook for 5-6 minutes to heat through. Serve with crusty bread, if liked.

Buttery
PRAWNS ON TOAST

AFFORDABILITY
1

1 Place a large frying pan over a medium heat and melt the butter with the cayenne pepper. Once the butter begins to froth slightly, add the prawns and cook for 2-3 minutes, stirring occasionally, until they are pink and cooked through.

2 Add the lemon juice, then stir in the chives and season to taste with salt and pepper. Spoon the prawns and their buttery juices on to the granary toast and serve immediately.

100 g (3½ oz) butter
pinch of cayenne pepper
300 g (10 oz) raw prawns,
   peeled
1 tablespoon lemon juice
2 tablespoons chopped chives
salt and pepper
4 slices of granary toast,
   to serve

Serves **4**
Prep time **5 minutes**
Cooking time **5 minutes**

STUDENT TIP

Online shopping helps to keep your budget in check, as you tend to buy what you need, rather than impulse buying in the shop. You can check your spend as you add items to your cyber trolley and, if you do get carried away, it's much easier to discard online items than retrace your steps in a supermarket.

STOVETOP SQUID
WITH OLIVES & TOMATOES

1. To prepare the squid, wash the tubes and pat dry on kitchen paper. If the tentacles are included, cut the tentacles away from the heads and wash and dry these too, discarding the heads. Cut the tubes across into thin rings.

2. Heat half the oil in a large shallow saucepan, frying pan or wok and fry the squid in two batches until they firm up into rings. Remove each batch with a slotted spoon and transfer to a plate. Set aside.

3. Add the onions to the pan or wok and fry for 3-4 minutes until the onions are beginning to colour. Add the garlic and fry for a further 1 minute. Return the squid and any juices on the plate to the pan or wok and add the tomatoes, olives, capers and the remaining oil. Cook for a further 2-3 minutes, stirring, until the tomatoes are hot and very slightly softened.

4. Add the lemon juice, season to taste with salt and pepper and sprinkle with the chopped parsley. Serve with warm grainy bread or ciabatta.

COOKING TIP
Try other types of fish instead of squid. Use the same weight of cubed skinless white fish such as cod, haddock or coley, or raw peeled prawns.

300 g (10 oz) squid tubes
4 tablespoons coconut or olive oil
2 red onions, thinly sliced
4 garlic cloves, thinly sliced
275 g (9 oz) cherry tomatoes, halved
50 g (2 oz) pitted black olives, halved
1 tablespoon capers, rinsed and drained
2 teaspoons lemon juice
salt and pepper
3 tablespoons chopped parsley, to garnish
warm grainy bread or ciabatta, to serve

Serves **4**
Prep time **15 minutes**
Cooking time **15 minutes**

MAKE FRIENDS WITH YOUR MICROWAVE

It might sound like a luxury for student accommodation but a microwave is very affordable and worth every penny: treat it well and keep it clean and you'll be rewarded with quick and easy meals day after day. From warming the milk for your morning porridge to blitzing eggs, reheating leftovers and rustling up a one-mug chocolate sponge (see opposite) for a quick sugar fix, this appliance will be one of the hardest working in the kitchen.

CHEAT'S SUPPERS

Obviously, nothing beats a home-cooked meal prepared with love and attention. However, if you're dashing home between college and the pub, it's perfectly acceptable to cheat a little – especially if that means you can enjoy a hearty fresh pasta dish rather than a cheese slice wedged between a couple of pieces of bread.

- Make a personal portion of mac and cheese by half filling a very large mug or small bowl with dry macaroni. Add a pinch of salt and cover the pasta with water. Place the mug or bowl in the microwave and blitz for 2 minutes at a time, stirring in between, until the pasta is cooked (add extra water if the pasta starts to dry). Stir in a little milk and a handful of grated Cheddar and microwave until the cheese is melted and has made a sauce.

- The same method applies to noodles - just use stock or sauce instead of water - and add some chopped peppers, baby corn, bean sprouts and any other vegetables you like towards the end of the cooking time.

- If you've got a sweet tooth, you might prefer to head straight for dessert, and a chocolate microwave mug cake will certainly hit the spot. Put 4 tablespoons each of caster sugar and self-raising flour and 2 tablespoons cocoa powder in the largest mug you can find. Mix, then add a beaten egg, a good drizzle of vegetable oil and 4 tablespoons milk. Mix and microwave for 5 minutes, or until the cake has risen fully.

KEEP IT CLEAN

There's nothing worse that opening the door of the microwave first thing in the morning and being greeted with the festering smells of last night's dinner - or worse, the congealed remains of last night's dinner. Shared kitchens can very quickly descend into chaos with standards of hygiene and cleanliness plummeting as the term progresses. Luckily, it's quick and easy to freshen up your microwave and all you need isa bowl and a lemon.

Pour some water into a large bowl and add the juice of half a lemon. Put the bowl in the microwave and cook for 3 minutes. Keeping the door shut, let the bowl stand for another 5 minutes so the steam lifts off the dirt. You'll now find it's really easy to wipe the inside with a soft damp cloth.

MUSHROOM
Stroganoff Ⓥ

1 tablespoon butter
2 tablespoons olive oil
1 onion, thinly sliced
4 garlic cloves, finely chopped
500 g (1 lb) chestnut
  mushrooms, sliced
2 tablespoons wholegrain
  mustard
250 ml (8 fl oz) crème fraîche
salt and pepper
3 tablespoons chopped parsley,
  to garnish

Serves **4**
Prep time **10 minutes**
Cooking time **10 minutes**

1 Melt the butter with the oil in a large frying pan, add the onion and garlic and cook until softened and starting to brown.

2 Add the mushrooms to the pan and cook until softened and starting to brown. Stir in the mustard and crème fraîche and just heat through. Season to taste with salt and pepper, then serve immediately, garnished with the chopped parsley.

AFFORDABILITY
1

TOMATO & CHICKPEA STEW

Vegan

1 Heat the oil in a large heavy-based saucepan. Add the onion, green pepper, garlic and ginger, and cook for 6-7 minutes until softened.

2 Stir in the cumin and coriander and cook for a further 1 minute. Add the tomato purée, stock, tomatoes and chickpeas, then cover and bring to the boil. Season generously with salt and pepper, reduce the heat and simmer for 8 minutes, or until thickened slightly and the tomatoes have softened. Ladle the stew into serving bowls and serve garnished with the chopped parsley.

2½ tablespoons olive oil
1 large onion, chopped
1 green pepper, cored, deseeded and chopped
1 garlic clove, chopped
2.5 cm (1 inch) piece of fresh root ginger, peeled and chopped
1 teaspoon ground cumin
1 teaspoon ground coriander
2 tablespoons tomato purée
500 ml (17 fl oz) hot vegetable stock (see page 15 for homemade)
4 large tomatoes, each cut into 8 wedges
2 x 400 g (13 oz) cans chickpeas, rinsed and drained
salt and pepper
2 tablespoons chopped parsley, to garnish

Serves **4**
Prep time **15 minutes**
Cooking time **20 minutes**

AFFORDABILITY

MUSTARDY SQUASH, CARROT & SWEET POTATO
CASSEROLE

3 tablespoons vegetable oil
1 red onion, roughly chopped
4 garlic cloves, chopped
750 g (1½ lb) butternut squash,
   peeled, deseeded and cut into
   bite-sized chunks
500 g (1 lb) sweet potatoes,
   peeled and cut into bite-sized
   chunks
2 carrots, cut into bite-sized
   chunks
125 ml (4 fl oz) dry white wine
1 teaspoon dried tarragon or
   rosemary
400 ml (14 fl oz) hot vegetable
   stock (see page 15 for
   homemade)
2 tablespoons wholegrain
   mustard
200 g (7 oz) spinach, washed,
   drained and shredded
salt and pepper
steamed couscous or rice,
   to serve

Serves **4**
Prep time **15 minutes**
Cooking time **30 minutes**

1   Heat the oil in a heavy-based saucepan. Cook the
    onion and garlic for 3-4 minutes, until softened.
    Add the squash, sweet potatoes and carrots and
    cook for a further 3-4 minutes until lightly golden.

2   Pour in the wine, add the tarragon or rosemary and
    cook until reduced by half. Add the stock and mustard
    to the pan, then season generously with salt and pepper,
    bring to the boil and simmer gently for 15 minutes,
    or until the vegetables are tender.

3   Tip the spinach into the pan and stir until wilted. Serve
    with steamed couscous or rice.

BROWN RICE,
MINT & HALOUMI PILAF

2 tablespoons olive oil
125 g (4 oz) haloumi cheese,
  cut into 1 cm (½ inch) chunks
1 large onion, chopped
1 celery stick, chopped
2 small courgettes, diced
1 teaspoon cumin seeds
¼ teaspoon dried red chilli
  flakes
150 g (5 oz) brown basmati rice
750 ml (1¼ pints) vegetable
  stock (see page 15 for
  homemade)
40 g (1½ oz) dates, chopped,
  or sultanas (optional)
1 tablespoon chopped mint
salt and pepper

Serves **2**
Prep time **15 minutes**
Cooking time **55 minutes**

1 Heat the oil in a frying pan. Add the haloumi and fry over a medium heat for 3-4 minutes until the cheese is turning golden, turning the pieces a couple of times for even browning. Lift out on to a plate with a slotted spoon.

2 Add the onion, celery and courgettes to the pan and fry for 8-10 minutes, stirring frequently, until golden. Stir in the spices and rice and cook, stirring frequently, for 1 minute.

3 Pour in the stock and bring to a gentle simmer. Reduce the heat to its lowest setting and cook for about 40 minutes, stirring frequently, until the rice is tender and all the liquid has been absorbed. Towards the end of the cooking time, pack the rice down flat with the back of the spoon so it plumps up evenly. If the mixture is dry before the rice is cooked, stir in a little hot water, but make sure all the water has cooked off so the rice is almost sticky.

4 Stir in the dates or sultanas, if using, the haloumi and the mint. Season to taste with salt and pepper before serving.

COOKING TIP
Pilafs are remarkably versatile. You can add other vegetables like diced aubergine or peppers instead of the courgette, chopped nuts or pine nuts for texture and other herbs like coriander or parsley. Substitute olives for the dried fruit if you prefer a more savoury flavour.

Spiced BLACK BEANS & CABBAGE

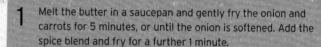

40 g (1½ oz) butter
1 large onion, chopped
150 g (5 oz) baby carrots, scrubbed
1 tablespoon ras el hanout spice blend (see tip for homemade)
500 ml (17 fl oz) vegetable stock (see page 15 for homemade)
200 g (7 oz) new potatoes, scrubbed and diced
400 g (13 oz) can black beans, rinsed and drained
175 g (6 oz) cabbage
salt (optional)

Serves **2**
Prep time **15 minutes**
Cooking time **30 minutes**

1 Melt the butter in a saucepan and gently fry the onion and carrots for 5 minutes, or until the onion is softened. Add the spice blend and fry for a further 1 minute.

2 Pour in the stock and bring to the boil. Reduce the heat to its lowest setting and stir in the potatoes and beans. Cover and cook gently for 15 minutes, or until the vegetables are tender and the juices slightly thickened.

3 Cut away the thick stalks from the cabbage and discard, then roll up the leaves and finely shred. Add to the pan and cook for a further 5 minutes. Season with salt, if necessary, and serve.

COOKING TIP
For a homemade ras el hanout spice blend, place ½ teaspoon each cumin, coriander and fennel seeds in a mortar and crush with a pestle. Add 1 teaspoon yellow mustard seeds and ¼ teaspoon each ground cinnamon and cloves and grind the spices together. Alternatively, use a small coffee or spice grinder to grind the spices.

AFFORDABILITY 1

Scrambled eggs
WITH SPINACH, GARLIC & RAISINS

15 g (½ oz) butter
1 shallot, chopped
1 small garlic clove, finely sliced
¼ teaspoon cumin seeds
1 tablespoon raisins
large handful of baby spinach leaves
2 eggs, beaten
salt and pepper
1 warm flatbread, to serve

Serves **1**
Prep time **5 minutes**
Cooking time **10 minutes**

1 Melt the butter in a small frying pan or saucepan. As soon as it starts to foam, add the shallot and fry for 3 minutes to soften. Add the garlic, cumin seeds and raisins and stir over a low heat for 1 minute.

2 Add the spinach and cook until the leaves start to wilt. Immediately tip in the eggs and cook, stirring constantly, until the eggs have lightly scrambled. Season to taste with salt and pepper and serve with the warm flatbread.

COOKING TIP
Don't be put off by the unusual combination of raisins and eggs. It really works well, giving the dish a slightly Middle Eastern flavour. A pinch of ground cumin or coriander can be used instead of the seeds, and a pinch of chilli is good if you like a fierier kick.

AKURI v

AFFORDABILITY 1

1 tablespoon butter
1 small red onion, finely
  chopped
1 green chilli, finely sliced
8 eggs, lightly beaten
1 tablespoon soured cream
1 tomato, skinned (see page 16)
  and finely chopped
1 tablespoon chopped fresh
  coriander
sea salt flakes
buttered toast, to serve

Serves **4**
Prep time **10 minutes**
Cooking time **10 minutes**

1 Heat the butter in a large nonstick frying pan, add the onion and chilli and cook for 2-3 minutes.

2 Add the eggs, soured cream, tomato and coriander and season with sea salt flakes. Cook over a low heat, stirring frequently, for 3-4 minutes until the eggs are lightly scrambled and set. Serve with buttered toast.

STUDENT TIP

Sign up for loyalty cards at all the big supermarkets and collect points for your shopping. You can choose to use these on your grocery bill, or swap them for vouchers or other deals. The value of points varies between retailers so check who's currently offering the best value.

Balsamic ROAST TOMATOES

12 plum tomatoes, about 700 g
  (1 lb 7 oz)
2 tablespoons olive oil
2 teaspoons balsamic vinegar
small bunch of basil, leaves torn
2 tablespoons pine nuts
1 small ciabatta
salt and pepper

Serves **4**
Prep time **5 minutes**
Cooking time **40-45 minutes**

1 Halve the tomatoes and arrange, cut-side uppermost, in a roasting tin. Drizzle with the oil and vinegar. Tear half the basil leaves over the top, add the pine nuts, and season with salt and pepper. Roast in a preheated oven, 180°C (350°F), Gas Mark 4, for 35-40 minutes until tender.

2 Cut the ciabatta in half lengthways then half again to give 4 quarters. Toast the cut side of the bread only, then transfer to serving plates and spoon the tomatoes on top. Tear the remaining basil leaves over the top and serve immediately.

AFFORDABILITY 1

TARRAGON MUSHROOM TOASTS Ⓥ

1 Toast the brioche slices lightly and keep warm.

2 Heat the butter in a frying pan and sauté the shallots, garlic and chilli, if using, for 1-2 minutes. Add the mushrooms and stir-fry over a medium heat for 6-8 minutes. Season well with salt and pepper, then remove from the heat and stir in the crème fraîche and herbs.

3 Spoon the mushrooms on to the toasted brioche and serve immediately, with an extra dollop of crème fraîche, if liked.

8 slices of brioche
150 g (5 oz) butter
2 banana shallots, finely chopped
3 garlic cloves, finely chopped
1 red chilli, deseeded and finely chopped (optional)
300 g (10 oz) mixed wild mushrooms, such as chanterelle, cep, girolle and oyster, or white mushrooms, trimmed and sliced
4 tablespoons crème fraîche, plus extra to garnish (optional)
2 tablespoons finely chopped tarragon
1 tablespoon finely chopped parsley
salt and pepper

Serves **4**
Prep time **15 minutes**
Cooking time **15 minutes**

AFFORDABILITY
2

Devilled MUSHROOMS (V)

1 tablespoon sunflower oil
4 tablespoons butter
6 spring onions, white parts
finely chopped and green
tops reserved
425 g (14 oz) white mushrooms,
sliced
2 tablespoons Worcestershire
sauce
2 teaspoons wholegrain
mustard
2 teaspoons tomato purée
a few drops of Tabasco sauce
(optional)
4 slices of crusty bread
salt and pepper

Serves **4**
Prep time **5 minutes**
Cooking time **10 minutes**

1 Heat the oil and butter in a frying pan. Add the white chopped spring onions and the mushrooms and fry for 3-4 minutes, stirring, until golden.

2 Stir in the Worcestershire sauce, mustard and tomato purée. Add 4 tablespoons water, the Tabasco sauce, if using, and a little salt and pepper. Cook for 2 minutes, stirring, until the sauce is beginning to thicken.

3 Toast the bread under a preheated hot grill and arrange on serving plates.

4 Stir the green spring onions tops through the mushrooms and cook for 1 minute, then spoon over the toast. Serve immediately.

AFFORDABILITY 1

CARROT & CABBAGE SLAW

AFFORDABILITY
1

1 Mix together the cabbage, carrots, spring onions, yogurt, mustard and lemon juice in a bowl and season with pepper to taste.

100 g (3½ oz) red cabbage, shredded
2 carrots, grated
3 spring onions, finely chopped
100 ml (3½ fl oz) natural yogurt
1 teaspoon wholegrain mustard
juice of 1 small lemon
pepper

Serves **4**
Prep time **15 minutes**

STUDENT TIP

Always check out the price per kilo of the different options when you buy fruit and veg in the supermarket. You might be shocked to find that a shrink-wrapped head of broccoli or pre-packaged courgettes could be up to twice the price per kilo of loose vegetables.

COURGETTE & HERB Risotto

4 tablespoons butter
2 tablespoons olive oil
1 large onion, finely chopped
2 garlic cloves, finely chopped
350 g (11½oz) risotto rice
200 ml (7 fl oz) white wine
1.5 litres (2½ pints) vegetable
  stock, heated to simmering
  (see page 15 for homemade)
200 g (7 oz) baby spinach
  leaves, chopped
100 g (3½ oz) courgettes, finely
  diced
50 g (2 oz) Parmesan cheese,
  finely grated
1 small handful of dill, mint and
  chives, roughly chopped
salt and pepper

Serves **4**
Prep time **10 minutes**
Cooking time **about
  20 minutes**

1 Melt the butter with the oil in a saucepan, add the onion and garlic and cook for about 3 minutes until softened. Add the rice and stir until coated with the butter mixture. Pour in the wine and cook rapidly, stirring, until it has evaporated.

2 Add the stock, a ladleful at a time, and cook, stirring constantly, until each addition has been absorbed before adding the next. Continue until all the stock has been absorbed and the rice is creamy and cooked but still retains a little bite - this will take around 15 minutes.

3 Stir in the spinach and courgettes and heat through for 3-5 minutes. Remove from the heat and stir in the Parmesan and herbs. Season to taste with salt and pepper and serve immediately.

AFFORDABILITY
2

BOSTON BAKED BEANS

1 Heat the oil in a heavy saucepan. Add the onion and cook over low heat for 5 minutes, or until softened. Add the celery and garlic and continue to cook for 1–2 minutes.

2 Add the tomatoes, stock and soy sauce. Bring to the boil, then reduce the heat to a fast simmer and cook for about 15 minutes until the sauce begins to thicken.

3 Add the sugar, mustard and beans and cook for a further 5 minutes or until the beans are heated through. Stir in the parsley and serve.

1 tablespoon vegetable oil
1 small red onion, finely chopped
2 celery sticks, finely chopped
1 garlic clove, crushed
150 g (5 oz) canned chopped tomatoes
150 ml (¼ pint) vegetable stock (see page 15 for homemade)
1 tablespoon dark soy sauce
1 tablespoon dark brown sugar
2 teaspoons Dijon mustard
200 g (7 oz) canned mixed beans, rinsed and drained
2 tablespoons chopped parsley

Serves **2**
Prep time **10 minutes**
Cooking time **30 minutes**

BRAIN BOWLS

As you're already at college or university, you must have done something right and earned your place through hard work and determination. However, there's no harm in giving your brain cells an extra boost every now and then – if nothing else, it might help to realign the balance after a few late nights on the booze. There are plenty of ingredients that will help with memory power, alertness and general wellbeing and a salad is by far the easiest way to rustle up a bowl of pure brainpower.

Here are a few brain-boosting ingredients:

- Spinach (beta carotene)
- Avocados (omega-3 fatty acid)
- Salmon, tuna and other oily fish (essential fatty acids)
- Eggs (vitamin B12)
- Broccoli (vitamin K)
- Tomatoes (antioxidants)
- Pumpkin seeds (zinc)

QUICK SALAD IDEAS

- **Niçoise bowl** Peeled and quartered boiled egg, tomatoes, green beans, tuna, Little Gem lettuce and boiled new potatoes.

- **Broccoli bowl** Steamed and cooled broccoli florets, green beans and petits pois mixed with a vinaigrette dressing.

- **Something fishy bowl** Steamed and cooled salmon fillet on a bed of baby spinach, sprinkled with pumpkin seeds and drizzled with balsamic vinegar and olive oil.

- **Cool as a cucumber bowl** Cubed avocado, cucumber, tomatoes and feta cheese mixed with a drizzle of olive oil and lemon juice. For a heartier meal, add some chopped, cooked chicken breast.

SOUPER SUPPER

Soup is another quick and easy way to rustle up a bowl of intelligence-boosting food. You can create a delicious, warming soup from virtually any ingredients and it's a particularly good way to use up leftover meat or vegetables (as long as they've been kept in the refrigerator). For example, leftover potatoes, sweet potato, squash, carrots, spinach or broccoli can be gently heated in a little stock or water and then blitzed with a handheld blender for an almost instant lunch. Sprinkle some health-giving seeds on your soup before serving.

Tomatoes also make an excellent base for soups and the addition of garlic, fresh basil and plenty of seasoning will make it a bowl of comfort food that's hard to beat.

Basic PIZZA DOUGH

7 g (¼ oz) fresh yeast or
  1 teaspoon dried yeast
pinch of caster sugar
500 g (1 lb) plain flour, plus
  extra for dusting
350 ml (12 fl oz) lukewarm
  water
1½ teaspoons salt
olive oil, for oiling

Serves **4**
Prep time **20 minutes, plus
  standing, resting and
  rising**

1 Dissolve the yeast in a bowl with the sugar, 2 tablespoons of the flour and 50 ml (2 fl oz) of the measured water. Leave to stand for 5 minutes until it starts to form bubbles.

2 Add the remaining water, the salt and half the remaining flour and stir with one hand until you have a paste-like mixture. Gradually add all the remaining flour, working the mixture until you have a moist dough. Shape the dough into a ball, cover with a moist tea towel and leave to rest in a warm place for 5 minutes.

3 Lightly dust a work surface with flour and knead the dough for 10 minutes, or until smooth and elastic. Shape into 4 equal-sized balls and place, spaced apart, on a lightly oiled baking sheet. Cover with a moist tea towel and leave to rise in a warm place for 1 hour. Use according to your recipe.

AFFORDABILITY 1

BASIC TOMATO SAUCE

1 Heat the oil in a heavy-based saucepan over a medium heat. Add the garlic and cook for 30 seconds, stirring, then add the tomatoes, sugar and basil, if using. Season lightly with salt and bring to the boil.

2 You now have two options. If you want a very light sauce to spoon over stuffed fresh pasta or if your sauce will be used in another recipe where it will undergo further cooking, simmer the sauce over a medium heat for 2-3 minutes. Alternatively, if you are aiming for a more robust, concentrated tomato sauce to stir into pasta, simmer the sauce over a low heat for 40-45 minutes until thick and rich. The sauce can be eaten chunky or blended with a handheld blender until smooth, then reheated.

2 teaspoons olive oil
1 garlic clove, finely chopped
1 kg (2 lb) canned chopped tomatoes
large pinch of caster sugar
5 basil leaves (optional)
salt

Serves **8**
Prep time **5 minutes**
Cooking time **5 minutes (for a light sauce), 45-50 minutes (for a robust sauce)**

EASY LAMB & BARLEY RISOTTO

SLOWLY DOES IT

CHICKEN & SWEET POTATO
WEDGES

JERK PORK WITH PINEAPPLE SALSA

MONDAY SAUSAGE STEW

BAKED SEAFOOD
WITH PAPRIKA

CHICKEN & CARAMELIZED ONION DHAL

1. Heat the oil in a large saucepan and fry the onions for 8-10 minutes, stirring frequently until deep golden. Using a splotted spoon, transfer half of the onions to a plate and reserve.

2. Add the urad dal to the pan with the stock, garlic, ginger, turmeric and cumin seeds. Bring to a gentle simmer and leave to cook, stirring frequently, for 1-1¼ hours until the lentils are tender and the mixture has a thick, soup-like consistency. If it starts to dry out, add a little water. Stir in the chicken and cook gently for 10 minutes.

3. Season to taste with plenty of pepper. Divide among serving bowls, spoon the reserved onions on top, and garnish with chopped coriander. Serve with lemon or lime wedges and warm flatbreads.

COOKING TIP
Urad dal is most widely available in health food and Indian stores. Red or black lentils can be used instead but these cook more quickly, so reduce the stock to 750 ml (1½ pints) and cook the lentils until tender, topping up with water if the mixture starts to dry out.

3 tablespoons vegetable oil
3 onions, chopped
200 g (7 oz) urad dal, rinsed
1 litre (1¾ pints) chicken or vegetable stock (see pages 11 or 15 for homemade)
2 garlic cloves, finely chopped
20 g (¾ oz) fresh root ginger, peeled and finely chopped
1 teaspoon ground turmeric
1 teaspoon cumin seeds
300-400 g (10-13 oz) boneless, skinless chicken breast, cut into large pieces
pepper
roughly chopped fresh coriander, to garnish

To serve
lemon or lime wedges
warm flatbreads

Serves **4**
Prep time **15 minutes**
Cooking time **1½-1¾ hours**

CHICKEN & SWEET POTATO
wedges

4 sweet potatoes, about 1.25 kg
(2½ lb) in total, scrubbed and
cut into thick wedges
4 boneless, skinless chicken
thighs, cut into chunks
1 red onion, cut into wedges
4 plum tomatoes, cut into
chunks
150 g (5 oz) chorizo sausage,
skinned and sliced or diced,
if very large
leaves from 3 sprigs of
rosemary
4 tablespoons olive oil
salt and pepper
watercress salad, to serve
(optional)

Serves **4**
Prep time **20 minutes**
35 minutes

1 Put the sweet potatoes in a large roasting tin with the chicken, onion and tomatoes. Tuck the chorizo in and around the sweet potatoes, then sprinkle with the rosemary and some salt and pepper. Drizzle with the oil.

2 Roast in a preheated oven, 200°C (400°F), Gas Mark 6, for about 35 minutes, turning once or twice, until the chicken is golden and cooked through and the sweet potato wedges are browned and tender. Spoon on to serving plates and serve with a watercress salad, if liked.

VARIATION
For mixed roots with fennel and chicken, use a mixture of 1.25 kg (2½ lb) baking potatoes, parsnips and carrots. Scrub the potatoes and peel the parsnips and carrots, then cut the root vegetables into wedges. Add to the roasting tin with the chicken as above. Sprinkle with 2 teaspoons fennel seeds, 1 teaspoon ground turmeric and 1 teaspoon paprika, then drizzle with 4 tablespoons olive oil and roast as above.

AFFORDABILITY **1**

West Indian CHICKEN TRAYBAKE

AFFORDABILITY
2

3 tablespoons vegetable or mild
  olive oil
2 onions, sliced
2 red peppers, cored, deseeded
  and sliced
2 teaspoons paprika
1 teaspoon ground cumin
4 garlic cloves, finely chopped
1 kg (2 lb) skinless, boned
  chicken thighs
300 ml (½ pint) chicken or
  vegetable stock (see pages
  11 or 15 for homemade)
400 g (13 oz) can coconut milk
6 fresh or frozen mini corncobs
4 tomatoes, cut into chunks
salt and pepper
chopped fresh coriander,
  to garnish
warm cornbread, to serve (see
  page 61 for homemade)

Serves **6**
Prep time **20 minutes**
Cooking time **1³/4 hours**

1 Heat 2 tablespoons of the oil in a roasting tin on the hob and gently fry the onions and red peppers for 10 minutes, stirring frequently, until golden. Stir in the spices and garlic. Add the remaining oil and the chicken thighs to the tin, turning them in the spicy mixture until lightly seared.

2 Add the stock and then the coconut milk, stirring the ingredients to combine. Push the corncobs down into the liquid and bring to a gentle simmer.

3 Cover with foil and bake in a preheated oven, 180°C (350°F), Gas Mark 4, for 1¼ hours.

4 Stir in the tomatoes and return to the oven, uncovered, for a further 15 minutes. Season to taste with salt and pepper and garnish with the chopped coriander. Serve with the warm cornbread.

COOKING TIP
Stir in 200 g (7 oz) frozen sweetcorn instead of the corn cobs if preferred. This is a dish to put on the centre of the table and let everyone help themselves. Serve with plenty of bread for mopping up the juices.

BALSAMIC BRAISED
PORK CHOPS

4 spare rib pork chops, about 750 g (1½ lb) in total
3 tablespoons balsamic vinegar
2 tablespoons light muscovado sugar
2 onions, thinly sliced
2 dessert apples, peeled, cored and quartered
2 tablespoons cornflour
3 teaspoons English mustard
200 ml (7 fl oz) boiling chicken stock (see page 11 for homemade)
chopped chives, to garnish (optional)

To serve
mashed potatoes
steamed Brussels sprouts

Serves **4**
Prep time **15 minutes**
7-8 hours

1 Preheat the slow cooker if necessary; see the manufacturer's instructions. Arrange the pork chops in the base of the slow cooker pot and spoon over the vinegar and sugar. Sprinkle the onions on top, then add the apples.

2 Put the cornflour and mustard in a mug and blend with a little cold water to make a smooth paste, then gradually stir in the stock until smooth and pour over the pork. Cover with the lid and cook on high for 30 minutes. Reduce the heat and cook on low for 6½-7½ hours until the pork is cooked through and tender.

3 Transfer the pork to serving plates, stir the sauce and spoon over the chops. Sprinkle with chopped chives, if liked. Serve with mashed potatoes and steamed Brussels sprouts.

VARIATION
For a cider-braised pork, prepare the pork chops as above, omitting the vinegar. Bring 200 ml (7 fl oz) dry cider to the boil in a saucepan. Make up the cornflour paste as above, then gradually stir in the boiling cider instead of the stock. Pour over the chops and continue as above.

Easy
LAMB & BARLEY
RISOTTO

20 g (¾ oz) mixed dried
    mushrooms
1 litre (1¾ pints) boiling
    vegetable stock (see page
    15 for homemade)
4 tablespoons cream sherry
    or fresh orange juice
1 onion, finely chopped
1 teaspoon ground cumin
2 garlic cloves, finely chopped
40 g (1½ oz) sultanas
125 g (4 oz) pearl barley
4 lamb chump chops, about
    150 g (5 oz) each
250 g (8 oz) pumpkin or
    butternut squash, peeled,
    deseeded and cut into 2 cm
    (¾ inch) dice
salt and pepper
chopped mint and parsley,
    to garnish
harissa, to serve

Serves **4**
Prep time **15 minutes**
 7-8 hours

1 Preheat the slow cooker if necessary; see the manufacturer's instructions. Put the dried mushrooms in the slow cooker pot, pour in the stock, then stir in the sherry or orange juice, onion, cumin, garlic, sultanas and barley and season with salt and pepper. Arrange the chops on top in a single layer, season with salt and pepper, then tuck the pumpkin or squash into the gaps between the chops. Press the chops and pumpkin or squash down lightly into the stock, then cover with the lid and cook on low for 7-8 hours until the lamb and vegetables are tender.

2 Lift the chops out of the slow cooker and break them into pieces. Stir the risotto well, then spoon on to serving plates, top with the chops and garnish with the chopped herbs. Serve with spoonfuls of harissa, if liked.

VARIATION
For a pumpkin & barley risotto, omit the lamb and use 400 g (13 oz) diced pumpkin. Cook as above, then add 125 g (4 oz) spinach to the risotto for the last 15 minutes of the cooking time. Serve topped with spoonfuls of Greek yogurt, chopped fresh mint and parsley and buttery fried flaked almonds.

MONDAY
SAUSAGE STEW

500 g (1 lb) pork chipolatas
1 onion, chopped
2 x 415 g (13½ oz) cans baked beans
2 tablespoons Worcestershire sauce
1 teaspoon dried mixed herbs
1 teaspoon Dijon mustard
200 ml (7 fl oz) boiling chicken stock (see page 11 for homemade)
300 g (10 oz) pumpkin or butternut squash, peeled, deseeded and cut into 2 cm (¾ inch) cubes
salt and pepper
garlic bread, to serve (optional)

....

Serves **4**
Preparation time **25 minutes**
Cooking time **7-8 hours**

....

1 Preheat the slow cooker if necessary; see the manufacturer's instructions. Grill the sausages on one side only.

2 Put the onion, baked beans and Worcestershire sauce in the slow cooker pot. Stir in the herbs, mustard and stock, then mix in the pumpkin or squash. Season with salt and pepper. Arrange the sausages on top, browned-sides uppermost, and press them into the liquid. Cover with the lid and cook on low for 7-8 hours until the sausages are cooked through and the pumpkin or squash is tender. Spoon into shallow serving bowls and serve with garlic bread, if liked.

VARIATION
For a chillied sausage stew, grill 500 g (1 lb) chillied pork sausages or plain chipolatas. Put the onion and 2 x 415 g (13½ oz) cans mixed beans in chilli sauce in the slow cooker pot, omitting the Worcestershire sauce, dried herbs and Dijon mustard. Mix in the stock and pumpkin or squash and cook as above. Garnish with 3 tablespoons chopped parsley.

SPICY PULLED GAMMON
with apricots

750 g (1½ lb) smoked gammon joint, well rinsed with cold water
300 ml (½ pint) apple or orange juice
2 cm (¾ inch) piece of fresh root ginger, peeled and grated, or 1 teaspoon ground ginger
2 tablespoons sweet chilli sauce
1 tablespoon brown sugar
6 fresh apricots, halved and stoned

To serve
6 seeded baps
100 g (3½ oz) watercress or rocket

Serves **6**
Prep time **10 minutes, plus standing**
Cooking time **4½ hours**

1   Put the gammon in a small roasting tin or baking dish and add the fruit juice. Cover with foil and bake in a preheated oven, 160°C (325°F), Gas Mark 3, for 4 hours, turning the gammon over about halfway through the cooking time.

2   Combine the ginger, chilli sauce and sugar in a mug and spread over the top of the gammon. Arrange the apricots around the meat, turning them in the fruit juice.

3   Return to the oven, uncovered, for a further 30 minutes until the glaze is stickily coating the meat and the apricots are tender. Leave to stand for 10 minutes.

4   Transfer the gammon to a board and shred the meat away from the joint using a fork.

5   To serve, halve the baps and drizzle a tablespoonful of the cooking juices over the bases. Sandwich the baps together with the watercress or rocket, apricots and shredded gammon. Serve warm.

COOKING TIP
If you don't have time to cook and serve the gammon on the same day, slow-cook it a day in advance, cool and chill overnight before finishing in a hot oven with the sticky glaze. Just make sure it's hot right through to the centre when you serve it. If you're not serving 6, chill the gammon in the refrigerator for several days and use up in salads, snacks and sandwiches.

Jerk PORK
WITH PINEAPPLE SALSA

750-875 g (1½-1¾ lb) pork
   shoulder joint
2 tablespoons powdered jerk
   spice mix
4 teaspoons light muscovado
   sugar
1 onion, roughly chopped
1 carrot, sliced
200 ml (7 fl oz) boiling chicken
   stock (see page 11 for
   homemade)
salt and pepper
boiled rice, to serve (optional)

Pineapple salsa
1 small pineapple, skinned,
   cored and finely chopped
2 teaspoons light muscovado
   sugar
1 large red chilli, halved,
   deseeded and finely chopped
grated zest of 1 lime

Serves **4**
Prep time **20 minutes**
5-6 hours

1 Preheat the slow cooker if necessary; see the manufacturer's instructions. Remove the string from the pork, then cut away the skin. Unroll and, if needed, make a slit in the meat so that it can be opened out to make a strip that is of an even thickness. Rub the pork all over with the jerk spice mix, sugar and salt and pepper. Put the pork in the slow cooker pot, then scatter the onion and carrot into the gaps around the pork. Pour in the stock, cover with the lid and cook on high for 5-6 hours until the meat is very tender and almost falls apart.

2 Meanwhile, put the pineapple in a bowl with the sugar, chilli and lime zest. Mix together, then cover with clingfilm and chill until the pork is ready.

3 Lift the pork out of the slow cooker pot, remove any fat, then shred the meat with 2 forks. Serve with the salsa and boiled rice, if liked.

PORK BELLY
& CHINESE CABBAGE WRAPS

1 large onion, sliced
1 large fennel bulb, sliced
1 kg (2 lb) lean pork belly, skinned
1½ teaspoons fennel seeds
1 teaspoon Chinese five-spice powder
½ Chinese cabbage, about 350 g (11½ oz), very thinly sliced
4 white or wholemeal wraps
4 tablespoons Asian plum sauce or hoisin sauce

Serves **4**
Prep time **10 minutes, plus standing**
Cooking time **4 hours**

1 Scatter the onion and fennel slices in a small roasting tin. Lay the piece of pork on top with the fattiest side uppermost. Sprinkle evenly with the fennel seeds and five-spice powder.

2 Cover with foil and bake in a preheated oven, 150°C (300°F), Gas Mark 2, for 4 hours, or until the meat is very tender, uncovering the tin for the last hour. Remove from the oven and lift the meat out of the tin. Tilt the tin so all the juices collect in one corner. Use a tablespoon or serving spoon to skim off the fat, leaving the meaty juices in the tin. Stir the cabbage into the juices, return the meat to the tin and leave in a warm place to stand for 10 minutes.

3 Meanwhile, lightly grill the wraps under a preheated hot grill until warmed through.

4 Transfer the meat to a board and slice as thinly as possible. Spread the centre of each wrap with plum or hoisin sauce, then scatter the shredded cabbage over the sauce and arrange the pork and cooked vegetables on top. Roll up and serve warm.

TURKEY & HAM CASEROLE

1   Season the flour with a little salt and pepper on a plate. Cut the turkey into small chunks and coat with the seasoned flour.

2   Melt the butter in a flameproof casserole and fry the turkey for 5 minutes, or until golden on all sides. Add the onions and celery to the casserole and fry for 4–5 minutes until softened. Tip in any remaining flour left on the plate. Pour in the stock, add the thyme and chilli powder and bring to a simmer, stirring.

3   Cover the casserole and cook in a preheated oven, 180°C (350°F), Gas Mark 4, for 45 minutes.

4   Stir the sweet potatoes and ham into the casserole and return to the oven for a further 30 minutes. Stir in the cranberries and crème fraîche and season to taste with salt and pepper. Return to the oven for a final 15 minutes before serving.

2 tablespoons plain flour
625 g (1¼ lb) turkey breast meat
50 g (2 oz) butter
2 onions, chopped
2 celery sticks, sliced
750 ml (1¼ pints) chicken stock (see page 11 for homemade)
1 tablespoon chopped thyme
½ teaspoon mild chilli powder
300 g (10 oz) sweet potatoes, scrubbed and cut into small chunks
350 g (11½ oz) ready-cooked ham in one piece, cut into dice
150 g (5 oz) cranberries
100 ml (3½ fl oz) crème fraîche
salt and pepper

Serves **6**
Prep time **20 minutes**
Cooking time **1¾ hours**

AFFORDABILITY

THREE MEALS
THREE WAYS

There are a number of recipes that you can cook that will open the door to a veritable smorgasbord of culinary treats. This is like multitasking to the extreme – you're essentially creating a number of different dishes while cooking one meal, and with just a few tweaks you can transform today's pasta sauce into tomorrow's pizza topping. The trick is to cook twice, or even three times, the amount you need for today's meal and then portion up the remainder to be used the following day, or frozen for another time entirely. We've started you off with a few ideas below.

BOLOGNESE SAUCE

1 Obviously for your first meal, you use this deliciously rich, meaty sauce as an accompaniment for pasta – be that the traditional spaghetti, or penne, fusilli, etc.

2 Use the second portion as a lasagne sauce. Technically, this is still one-pot cooking as the sauce is already prepared and you're cooking the lasagne in just one dish. Simply spoon a layer of sauce on the bottom of the dish, arrange a layer of lasagne sheets on top and then cover with some white sauce – repeat three times for a sturdy lasagne that doesn't run away over the plate. Bake in a preheated oven, 180°C (350°F), Gas Mark 4, for about 30 minutes.

3 For chilli con carne, add 1 teaspoon chilli powder and a drained and rinsed can of red kidney beans to the third portion of sauce. Heat thoroughly and serve with boiled rice.

ROAST CHICKEN

1 Transform your Sunday roast into a Monday curry: add a little oil to a pan with a chopped onion and fry until softened. Add 1/2 teaspoon each of ground turmeric, ground coriander and chilli powder and stir in a 400 g (13 oz) can of chopped tomatoes. Cook for a few minutes then stir in chopped leftover cooked chicken and cook for about 10 minutes. Finish with a swirl of yogurt or crème fraîche.

2 Shred some of the leftover cooked chicken, mix together in a bowl with some chopped spring onion, red pepper and cucumber and soy sauce. Use this mixture to fill wontons or wraps for a healthy lunch.

3 Make a super-quick chicken Caesar salad by mixing together roughly chopped leftover cooked chicken, cos lettuce and shavings of Parmesan cheese in a bowl. Serve with ranch dressing and croutons – and anchovies, if you have a jar in the cupboard.

PULLED PORK

1 This is the perfect meal to prepare for a dinner party or summer lunch with friends as you can serve the same dish a number of different ways at the same time. Firstly, shred some of the meat, mix with a potent barbecue sauce and serve in warmed buns – delicious.

2 Next, pile some pork and chopped peppers and chillies into warmed tacos for a Mexican-inspired take on the classic dish.

3 Finally, spread out a couple of pizza bases, spoon over passata and torn mozzarella and sprinkle some shredded pork on top before cooking.

FEIJOADA
WITH STICKY RIBS

1 tablespoon vegetable or mild olive oil

100 g (3½ oz) smoked streaky bacon, roughly diced

2 red onions, roughly chopped

3 garlic cloves, finely chopped

1 green chilli, deseeded and finely chopped

2 x 400 g (13 oz) cans black beans, rinsed and drained

500 ml (17 fl oz) chicken or vegetable stock (see pages 11 or 15 for homemade)

200 g (7 oz) can chopped tomatoes

1 tablespoon red or white wine vinegar

500 g (1 lb) pork ribs, sold as individual ribs or in one piece

2 tablespoons light or dark muscovado sugar

½ teaspoon paprika

salt and pepper

Serves **3-4**
Prep time **15 minutes**
Cooking time 1**½ hours**

1 Heat the oil in a large, shallow flameproof casserole. Add the bacon and onions and fry gently for 5 minutes, stirring frequently, until the onions are beginning to colour. Add the garlic and chilli and fry for a further 1 minute.

2 Stir in the beans, stock, tomatoes, 1 teaspoon of the vinegar and a little salt and pepper and bring to the boil. Reduce the heat slightly and cook for 10-15 minutes, stirring frequently, until the liquid has thickened to make a thick sauce.

3 If the pork ribs are in one piece, cut them into 3 or 4 rib pieces. Place the ribs on top of the stew. Combine the sugar with the paprika and the remaining vinegar and spoon half over the ribs, spreading it with the back of a teaspoon.

4 Cover the casserole and bake in a preheated oven, 160°C (325°F), Gas Mark 3, for 30 minutes. Remove the lid and spread the pork with the remaining paprika mixture. Return to the oven, uncovered, for a further 45 minutes.

AFFORDABILITY **2**

Beef & coconut
STEW

1 tablespoon plain flour or
  cornflour
¼ teaspoon ground turmeric
500 g (1 lb) diced braising beef
2 tablespoons vegetable or
  mild olive oil
1 large onion, chopped
1 green pepper, cored,
  deseeded and thinly sliced
2 teaspoons yellow mustard
  seeds
1 teaspoon fenugreek seeds
  (optional)
8-10 cardamom pods
¼ teaspoon dried red chilli
  flakes
4 garlic cloves, finely chopped
400 ml (14 fl oz) can coconut
  milk
salt and pepper
chunks of bread or boiled
  basmati rice, to serve

Serves **4**
Prep time **20 minutes**
Cooking time **1½-1¾ hours**

1 On a dinner plate, mix together the flour or cornflour, turmeric and a little salt and pepper. Add the beef and turn in the flour mixture until coated.

2 Heat 1 tablespoon of the oil in a large saucepan. Add half the beef and fry quickly for 3-4 minutes, stirring, until browned. Lift out of the pan with a slotted spoon and return to the plate. Add the remaining beef and cook for 3-4 minutes, stirring, until browned, then transfer the beef to the plate.

3 Add the remaining oil to the pan with the onion and green pepper and fry gently for 4-5 minutes. Return the beef to the pan with any excess flour on the plate. Add the spices and garlic and cook for 2 minutes. Add the coconut milk and heat until barely simmering. Cover and cook very gently for about 1¼-1½ hours until the beef is very tender. Take care not to boil the meat or it'll make it tough.

4 Season to taste with salt and pepper. Divide among serving bowls and serve with chunks of bread or boiled basmati rice.

AFFORDABILITY
2

1 onion, finely chopped
1 red pepper, cored, deseeded
and diced
2 garlic cloves, finely chopped
400 g (13 oz) can chopped
tomatoes
150 ml (¼ pint) dry white wine
or fish stock (see page 104
for homemade)
large pinch of paprika
2 sprigs of thyme
1 tablespoon olive oil
400 g (13 oz) pack frozen
seafood (prawns, mussels,
squid), defrosted
salt and pepper
chopped parsley, to garnish
cooked pasta, such as
tagliatelle, to serve

Serves **4**
Preparation time **15 minutes**
Cooking time **5½-7½ hours**

BAKED
SEAFOOD
WITH PAPRIKA

1 Preheat the slow cooker if necessary; see the
manufacturer's instructions. Put the onion, red pepper,
garlic and tomatoes into the slow cooker pot, then add
the wine or stock, paprika, thyme, oil and a little salt
and pepper. Cover with the lid and cook on low for
5-7 hours.

2 Rinse the seafood with cold water, drain and then stir
into the slow cooker pot. Re-cover and cook on high for
30 minutes, or until piping hot. Garnish with the
chopped parsley and serve with cooked pasta.

STUDENT TIP

It might sound obvious, but don't wait
until you're ready to cook to check you
have all the ingredients needed for a
recipe. Go through the cupboards in the
morning so you can pick up any missing
items while you're out and about.

SWEET STUFF & DRINKS

SUMMER FRUIT GRATIN

CHOCOLATE FUDGE BROWNIE

SYRUP SPONGE PUDDING

TROPICAL FRUIT SMOOTHIE

Bircher MUESLI (V)

1 Mix together the buckwheat flakes, milk, apple juice and apple in a bowl. Cover with clingfilm and leave to soak overnight.

2 To serve, stir the honey, dried fruit and nuts into the muesli mixture. Spoon into serving bowls, then top with the poached or canned fruit.

VARIATION
You can try this recipe with any of your favourite dried fruit and nuts or you can add a bit of dried coconut for a tropical flavour.

200 g (7 oz) buckwheat flakes
300 ml (½ pint) milk
100 ml (3½ fl oz) apple juice
1 apple, peeled and grated

To serve
2 tablespoons clear honey
100 g (3½ oz) ready-to-eat
  dried fruit, such as mango,
  apricots or sultanas
100 g (3½ oz) hazelnuts,
  toasted and roughly chopped
poached or canned fruit, such
  as peaches or berries

Serves **4**
Prep time **5 minutes, plus
  overnight soaking**

AFFORDABILITY 2

BUCKWHEAT PORRIDGE

200 g (7 oz) buckwheat flakes
1 ripe banana, chopped
½ teaspoon ground cinnamon
100 g (3½ oz) sultanas
200 ml (7 fl oz) milk
200 ml (7 fl oz) water

To serve
clear honey
200 g (7 oz) mixed berries

Serves **4**
Prep time **5 minutes**
Cooking time **5 minutes**

1 Place all the ingredients in a saucepan over a low heat and bring to a simmer, then cook gently for 3-4 minutes until the buckwheat flakes are tender.

2 Blend briefly with a handheld blender, then spoon into serving bowls, drizzle with a little honey and serve with mixed berries.

VARIATION
Replace the banana with a chopped pear and serve with chopped toasted walnuts and honey.

STUDENT TIP

When it comes to shopping for everyday items, a quick and easy way to save money is to switch from big brands to own brands. Breakfast cereals, condiments, drinks and cleaning products are just some of the own-brand shopping-trolley staples that will slash your budget.

PUMPKIN SEED & APRICOT
Muesli Ⓥ

50 g (2 oz) jumbo rolled oats
1 tablespoon sultanas or raisins
1 tablespoon pumpkin seeds
1 tablespoon chopped almonds
2 tablespoons chopped ready-
to-eat dried apricots
2 tablespoons fruit juice, such
as apple or orange juice, or
water
2 small apples, peeled and
grated
3 tablespoons milk or natural
yogurt, to serve

Serves **2**
Prep time **5 minutes**
Cooking time **5 minutes**

1 Place the oats, sultanas or raisins, pumpkin seeds, almonds and apricots in a bowl with the fruit juice or water. Add the apple and mix well. Spoon into serving bowls and serve topped with milk or yogurt.

AFFORDABILITY
2

STUDENT TIP
Whether you're lucky enough to have a dishwasher in your digs or you have to get down and dirty with the dishes, always rinse pots, pans and plates as soon as they've been used. That way, if the dishwashing fairies turn up late for their shift, the food won't have dried like a layer of cement and washing up will be easier.

BAKED HONEY
PEACHES

50 g (2 oz) butter, plus extra
for greasing
4 large peaches, halved and
stoned
50 g (2 oz) flaked almonds
75 g (3 oz) clear honey
ground cinnamon, for dusting
soured cream, to serve

Serves **4**
Prep time **5 minutes**
Cooking time **10-15 minutes**

1 Grease a shallow baking dish with butter. Place the
peaches, skin-side down, in the prepared baking dish.
Dot the peaches with butter, then sprinkle with the
almonds, drizzle with the honey and dust with a little
cinnamon.

2 Bake in a preheated oven, 200ºC (400ºF), Gas Mark
6, for 10-15 minutes until the peaches are start to
colour and the almonds have lightly browned. Serve
the peaches with the juices drizzled over, and topped
with a spoonful of soured cream.

RHUBARB & GINGER SLUMP (V)

750 g (1½ lb) rhubarb, trimmed
and cut into chunks
1 tablespoon self-raising flour
50 g (2 oz) granulated sugar
2 pieces of stem ginger in
syrup, drained and chopped,
plus 2 tablespoons syrup from
the jar

Topping
100 g (3½ oz) self-raising flour
75 g (3 oz) butter, softened
75 g (3 oz) granulated sugar
4 tablespoons milk
1 egg, beaten

Serves **4-6**
Prep time **10 minutes**
Cooking time **30 minutes**

AFFORDABILITY **2**

1 Place the rhubarb, flour, sugar, chopped ginger and syrup in a shallow ovenproof dish and toss together. Cover with foil and place in a preheated oven, 190ºC (375ºF), Gas Mark 5, for 3 minutes.

2 Meanwhile, make the topping. Place all the ingredients in a food processor and blend until smooth. Alternatively, rub the butter into the dry ingredients with your fingertips and then stir in the milk and beaten egg.

3 Uncover the rhubarb and spoon over the topping. Return to the oven for a further 25 minutes, or until the topping is golden and cooked through.

VARIATION
For rhubarb and ginger fools, whisk 200 ml (7 fl oz) double cream until soft peaks form, then stir in 1 tablespoon icing sugar. Gently stir in 125 g (4 oz) canned rhubarb, drained and chopped, and divide among serving bowls. Crumble 1 ginger biscuit over each portion and serve immediately.

APPLE & SALTED CARAMEL
Pudding Ⓥ

4 large tart dessert apples,
  such as Cox's
1 tablespoon lemon juice
5 tablespoons demerara sugar
125 g (4 oz) ready-made
  caramel sauce
¼ teaspoon sea salt flakes
50 g (2 oz) unsalted butter,
  very soft
4 thick slices white bread,
  crusts removed
pouring cream or ice cream,
  to serve

Serves **4**
Prep time **20 minutes**
Cooking time **40 minutes**

1 Peel, core and slice the apples. Put the apples in a pie dish, add the lemon juice and 2 tablespoons of the sugar and mix the ingredients together. Cover with foil and bake in a preheated oven, 190°C (375°F), Gas Mark 5, for 30 minutes until the apples are very tender.

2 Drizzle the caramel sauce over the apples with a teaspoon so it's fairly evenly distributed. Pinch the sea salt flakes between your fingers to crumble them up and sprinkle over the caramel.

3 Generously butter the bread slices with half the butter. Cut into triangles and arrange over the filling, buttered-side up. Sprinkle with the remaining sugar and dot with the remaining butter.

4 Bake for a further 10 minutes, uncovered, until the bread is crisped and heated through. If you like, pop the dish under a preheated hot grill for a few minutes until the surface is deep golden, but watch closely as it will quickly toast! Serve with pouring cream or ice cream.

AFFORDABILITY
2

CHOCOLATE FUDGE BROWNIE

200 g (7 oz) butter
200 g (7 oz) plain dark
  chocolate, chopped
175 g (6 oz) soft dark brown
  sugar
150 g (5 oz) caster sugar
4 eggs, beaten
50 g (2 oz) ground almonds
75 g (3 oz) plain flour
vanilla ice cream, to serve
  (optional)

Serves **8**
Prep time **10 minutes, plus
  cooling**
Cooking time **30 minutes**

1 Melt the butter and chocolate in a shallow ovenproof dish, about 23 cm (9 inches) across, over a low heat. Remove from the heat and leave to cool for a couple of minutes.

2 Beat together the sugars and eggs in a bowl, then stir in the chocolate mixture followed by the almonds and flour.

3 Wipe the rim of the ovenproof dish with a damp piece of kitchen paper to neaten, then pour in the chocolate mixture. Bake in a preheated oven, 180ºC (350ºF), Gas Mark 4, for 25 minutes, or until just set. Serve warm with vanilla ice cream, if liked.

AFFORDABILITY
2

SYRUP SPONGE
Pudding

1. Grease a 1.2 litre (2 pint) pudding basin with butter. Place all the ingredients, except the golden syrup, in a food processor and blend until smooth. Spoon 4 tablespoons of the golden syrup into the bottom of the prepared pudding basin, then add the pudding mixture and smooth the surface with a knife.

2. Cover with microwave-proof clingfilm and pierce the film a couple of times with a sharp knife. Cook in a microwave oven on medium heat for about 12 minutes. Test to see if it is cooked by inserting a skewer into the pudding; it should come out clean.

3. Leave to rest for 3 minutes, then turn out on to a deep plate and spoon over the remaining golden syrup. Serve with cream or custard.

175 g (6 oz) butter, softened, plus extra for greasing
175 g (6 oz) caster sugar
175 g (6 oz) self-raising flour
1 teaspoon baking powder
3 eggs
1 teaspoon vanilla extract
3 tablespoons milk
finely grated zest of ½ lemon
6 tablespoons golden syrup
cream or custard, to serve

Serves **6**
Prep time **5 minutes, plus resting**
Cooking time **15 minutes**

AFFORDABILITY **2**

Prune CLAFOUTIS (V)

butter, for greasing
3 eggs
125 g (4 oz) caster sugar
50 g (2 oz) plain flour
150 ml (¼ pint) double cream
150 ml (¼ pint) milk
1 teaspoon vanilla extract
75 g (3 oz) pitted soft prunes

Serves **4**
Prep time **10 minutes**
Cooking time **20-25 minutes**

1 Lightly grease a shallow ovenproof dish with butter. Whisk together the eggs and sugar in a bowl until pale, frothy and tripled in volume. Sift the flour into the bowl and lightly fold in. Add the cream, milk and vanilla extract and mix until just combined.

2 Pour into the prepared ovenproof dish and bake in a preheated oven, 190°C (375°F), Gas Mark 5, for 5 minutes, or until the surface is just starting to set. Scatter over the prunes, then return to the oven for a further 15-20 minutes until the clafoutis is risen and golden.

AFFORDABILITY 2

CRUNCHY BERRY *Brûlée*

250 g (8 oz) mascarpone cheese
300 ml (½ pint) ready-made fresh custard
150 g (5 oz) mixed berries
100 g (3½ oz) caster sugar
1½ tablespoons water

Serves **4**
Prep time **5 minutes**
Cooking time **15 minutes**

1 Beat the mascarpone in a bowl until smooth. Gently stir in the custard. Transfer the mixture to a serving dish and scatter the berries over the top.

2 Place the sugar and measured water in a small heavy-based saucepan and slowly bring to the boil, carefully swirling the pan from time to time. Keep cooking until the sugar dissolves, then turns a deep caramel colour. Pour over the berries and leave for a few minutes to harden.

VARIATION

For a melting berry yogurt, place 200 g (7 oz) mixed berries in a serving dish. Spoon over 300 ml (½ pint) natural yogurt, then sprinkle with 75 g (3 oz) soft dark brown sugar. Chill in the refrigerator for 20-25 minutes until the sugar has melted.

AFFORDABILITY 2

PASSION FRUIT & MANGO MESS

1 Whisk the cream with the icing sugar in a bowl until it just holds its shape.

2 Gently stir in the meringue, most of the mango and a little of the passion fruit pulp. Spoon into glasses and top with the remaining fruit.

VARIATION

For a passion fruit and mango cream, peel, stone and chop 1 mango and divide among 4 glasses. Whisk 1 egg yolk with 2 tablespoons caster sugar in a bowl until very frothy and pale, then stir in the pulp of 2 passion fruit. Whisk 200 ml (7 fl oz) double cream in a separate bowl until soft peaks form, then stir into the egg mixture and whisk until thickened. Gently stir in 1 tablespoon orange liqueur and 75 g (3 oz) crushed meringues. Spoon over the mango and top with a little more chopped fruit, if liked.

300 ml (½ pint) double cream
2-3 tablespoons icing sugar
4 meringue nests, crushed
1 mango, peeled, stoned and sliced
1 passion fruit, halved

Serves **4**
Prep time **10 minutes**

AFFORDABILITY
1

Crunchy
PEAR CRUMBLE

1 Place the pears in a shallow ovenproof dish with the sugar, cinnamon and measured water and stir together. Cover with foil and place in a preheated oven, 190°C (375°F), Gas Mark 5, for 5 minutes.

2 Meanwhile, make the crumble topping. Place the sugar in a food processor with the cinnamon, oats, flour and butter and pulse until the mixture resembles fine breadcrumbs. Alternatively, rub the butter into the dry ingredients with your fingertips. Stir the golden syrup into the topping mixture.

3 Remove the pears from the oven, uncover and scatter the topping over them. Return to the oven for a further 20-25 minutes until bubbling and lightly browned. Serve warm with custard.

VARIATION
For sautéed pears with crunchy topping, heat 25 g (1 oz) butter in a frying pan. Add 6 pears, peeled, quartered and cored, and cook for 5 minutes, turning often, until golden all over. Stir in ½ teaspoon ground cinnamon and 6 tablespoons orange juice and cook until the liquid bubbles away. Divide among serving bowls, then scatter with 6 crushed flapjack biscuits mixed with 25 g (1 oz) chopped pecan nuts. Spoon over natural yogurt or whipped cream to serve.

6 pears, peeled, cored and chopped
2 tablespoons soft light brown sugar
½ teaspoon ground cinnamon
4 tablespoons water
custard, to serve

Topping
75 g (3 oz) soft light brown sugar
½ teaspoon ground cinnamon
125 g (4 oz) rolled oats
75 g (3 oz) plain flour
75 g (3 oz) butter
1 tablespoon golden syrup

Serves **6**
Prep time **10 minutes**
Cooking time **25-30 minutes**

ONE-POT ENTERTAINING

Entertaining at home doesn't have to entail long days sweating in the kitchen, arranging napkins into intricate shapes and trying to rustle up a matching 64-piece bone china dinner service. You can make it as laid back and low key as you like – after all, many students survive college on a diet of beans on toast, caffeine and alcohol so no one is going to judge your cooking or hosting skills too harshly. However, you probably want everyone to enjoy the meal so it's a good idea not to attempt a brand new recipe when you're entertaining eight people. Choose something you've made before and are confident cooking; that way you can relax and enjoy the evening too.

One-pot entertaining has a number of obvious benefits – less clutter on the worktops, less washing up and much less chance of spectacular failure. It's harder to overcook or burn a one-pot meal, as you just have the one dish to think about, plus you tend to add all – or most of – the ingredients at the same time, so there's less chance of forgetting something vital and spoiling the meal.

Don't forget to check if anyone is vegetarian: if they are, you'll need to decide whether to cook a meat-free meal or cook something different for your veggie mates. Likewise, if anyone has food allergies, intolerances – or is just plain fussy – it's better to find out before you're about to serve dinner.

TOP TIPS FOR A TOP NIGHT

- Plan ahead - check the timings for preparation and cooking and make sure you have the right amount of each ingredient.

- Buy a few nibbles or some bread and dips to serve as a starter. This will take the pressure off you when you're cooking.

- Don't forget to preheat the oven so it's at the right temperature when you're ready to start cooking.

- Are you serving sides or bread with the meal? Don't forget to prepare these so they're ready at the same time as the main course.

- Check meat and fish are cooked through thoroughly before serving - you don't want to give your mates food poisoning.

- Create a playlist for the evening. That way, you won't have to get up and change the music in the middle of the meal.

- Check you have enough plates, cutlery and glasses well in advance.

- If you only have a small fridge, use a cool box and some ice packs for storing drinks - reserve fridge space for the food.

ROAST PLUMS
WITH STAR ANISE Ⓥ

500 g (1 lb) plums
⅛ teaspoon ground cinnamon
  or ginger
1 tablespoon broken star anise
  pieces
3 tablespoons demerara sugar
2 teaspoons lemon juice
50 g (2 oz) unsalted butter
vanilla ice cream, to serve

Serves **4**
Prep time **5 minutes**
Cooking time **20 minutes**

1 Halve and stone the plums and arrange, cut-sides face up, in a shallow ovenproof dish or roasting tin.

2 Using your fingers, sprinkle the cinnamon or ginger over the plums. Arrange the star anise pieces on top, breaking them further if the pieces are fairly intact so you have enough for most of the plums.

3 Sprinkle with the sugar and then drizzle with the lemon juice. Dot a small piece of butter on to each plum. Pour 3 tablespoons water into the dish or tin.

4 Bake in a preheated oven, 200°C (400°F), Gas Mark 6, for about 20 minutes until the plums are just tender. The time will vary depending on the ripeness of the plums. Divide the plums among serving plates and drizzle with the pan juices. Serve with vanilla ice cream.

BANANA CARAMEL
Puffs

AFFORDABILITY
2

1 Heat the sugar and measured water in a large ovenproof frying pan until golden and caramel coloured. Carefully add the butter and swirl around the pan until melted.

2 Meanwhile, cut out 4 rounds from the pastry using a 7 cm (3 inch) cookie cutter or glass.

3 Carefully arrange the banana slices in 4 circles in the caramel, then place a pastry round on top of each. Place in a preheated oven, 220°C (425°F), Gas Mark 7, for 15 minutes, or until the pastry is puffed and cooked through. Use a spatula to turn out of the pan and drizzle with the remaining sauce.

VARIATION
For banana and caramel pots, slice 2 bananas and divide among serving bowls. Whisk 150 ml (¼ pint) double cream in a bowl until soft peaks form, then stir in 1 tablespoon dulce de leche or other caramel sauce. Spoon over the banana, then drizzle with more dulce de leche and top with chopped pecans.

150 g (5 oz) soft light brown sugar
50 ml (2 fl oz) water
25 g (1 oz) butter
300 g (10 oz) ready-rolled puff pastry
2 bananas, sliced

Serves **4**
Prep time **5 minutes**
Cooking time **25 minutes**

SWEET AVOCADO CREAM
with mixed berries

3 large ripe avocados
finely grated zest and juice
  of 1 lime
75 g (3 oz) caster sugar
3 tablespoons single cream
1 egg white
mixed fresh berries, such as
  blackberries and raspberries,
  to decorate

....

Serves **4**
Prep time **10 minutes, plus
  chilling**

....

1 Halve and stone the avocados and scoop the flesh into a food processor or blender. Add the lime zest and juice and half the sugar and blend to a smooth purée. Blend in the cream.

2 Whisk the egg white in a thoroughly clean bowl until peaking. Gradually whisk in the remaining sugar, a teaspoonful at a time. Stir the egg white mixture gently into the avocado purée and spoon into serving dishes. Chill in the refrigerator. When you are ready to serve, divide among serving bowls and scatter the berries on top.

COOKING TIP
If you don't have a blender or food processor, mash the avocado as smoothly as possible with a potato masher before stirring in the cream. It's easiest to mash the avocados on a flat plate or in a pan. This will only work if the avocados are properly ripe.

Creamy
CHOCOLATE PUDDING

75 g (3 oz) granulated sugar
3 tablespoons cornflour
25 g (1 oz) cocoa powder
3 eggs
500 ml (17 fl oz) milk
75 g (3 oz) milk chocolate,
   chopped

To serve
whipped cream
grated milk chocolate

Serves **4**
Prep time **10 minutes, plus
   freezing**
Cooking time **10 minutes**

1 Place the sugar, cornflour and cocoa powder in a heatproof bowl and whisk in the eggs. Bring the milk to the boil in a saucepan, then whisk a little of it into the egg mixture. Transfer the cocoa mixture to the saucepan, stir well and cook for 3–5 minutes, stirring continuously, until thickened.

2 Place the chopped chocolate in the bowl, sieve the chocolate custard on top and stir until smooth. Cover the surface with clingfilm to prevent a skin forming, then place in the freezer for 15 minutes, stirring occasionally, until cool.

3 When the chocolate custard is cool, divide among serving bowls, top with whipped cream and sprinkle with grated chocolate.

VARIATION
For creamy chocolate truffles, bring 75 ml (3 fl oz) double cream to the boil in a small heavy-based saucepan. Place 150 g (5 oz) chopped plain dark chocolate in a heatproof bowl with 25 g (1 oz) butter. Pour over the cream and stir until smooth. Place in the freezer for 15 minutes, stirring occasionally, until the mixture has set. Use a teaspoon to scoop out pieces of the mixture, form into balls and roll in cocoa powder to serve.

AFFORDABILITY
1

PEACH & RASPBERRY *Melba* Ⓥ

AFFORDABILITY 2

1 Place the measured water, sugar and vanilla extract in a saucepan, cook over a low heat until the sugar dissolves, then cook over a high heat for 5-10 minutes until syrupy.

2 Add the peach halves and cook for a further 5 minutes, or until tender, then leave to cool. Remove the skins and thinly slice the peaches.

3 Arrange the peach slices, ice cream and half the raspberries in sundae glasses. Press the remaining raspberries through a sieve set over a bowl to make a coulis. Drizzle the coulis over the top of the sundaes and serve with biscuit curls.

250 ml (8 fl oz) water
125 g (4 oz) caster sugar
1 teaspoon vanilla extract
4 peaches, halved and stoned
8 scoops of vanilla ice cream
125 g (4 oz) raspberries
biscuit curls, to serve

Serves **4**
Prep time **5 minutes, plus cooling**
Cooking time **10-15 minutes**

VARIATION
For baked peaches and raspberries, place 4 halved and stoned peaches in an ovenproof dish. Pour over 6 tablespoons orange juice and add 2 tablespoons orange liqueur, if liked. Dot a little butter on each peach, then sprinkle with 2 tablespoons caster sugar. Place in a preheated oven, 200°C (400°F), Gas Mark 6, for 15 minutes, then scatter over 100 g (3½ oz) raspberries and return to the oven for a further 3 minutes, or until the peaches are tender and lightly caramelized. Serve with vanilla ice cream.

WHITE CHOCOLATE RISOTTO WITH RASPBERRIES

1 Put the milk in a large saucepan and heat gently until it starts to rise up in the pan. Add the rice and vanilla extract and reduce the heat to its lowest setting.

2 Stirring almost continuously, cook the risotto for about 15-20 minutes until the consistency is creamy and the rice is tender but retains a little bite. If the rice starts to dry out before the rice is cooked, add a dash more milk or water. As soon as the rice is cooked, remove the pan from the heat.

3 Break 75 g (3 oz) of the chocolate into pieces and stir into the rice until it's melted. Stir in half the raspberries until they're warmed through in the heat of the rice. Spoon into small serving bowls and scatter the remaining raspberries on top. Grate the remaining chocolate on top to serve.

VARIATION
Try other fruits such as sliced strawberries, blueberries or blackberries instead of the raspberries.

450 ml (¾ pint) milk
125 g (4 oz) risotto rice
1 teaspoon vanilla extract
100 g (3½ oz) white chocolate
150 g (5 oz) raspberries

Serves **4**
Prep time **20 minutes**
Cooking time **15-20 minutes**

CHOC CHIP ICE CREAM *Sandwiches* Ⓥ

150 g (5 oz) butter, softened
100 g (3½ oz) granulated sugar
100 g (3½oz) soft light brown
  sugar
1 egg, beaten
175 g (6 oz) plain flour
1 teaspoon baking powder
1 teaspoon vanilla extract
100 g (3½ oz) mixed plain dark,
  milk and white chocolate
  chips
4 scoops of vanilla ice cream

Serves **4 (with leftover
  cookies)**
Prep time **10 minutes, plus
  cooling**
Cooking time **10 minutes**

1 Line a baking sheet with greaseproof paper. Beat the butter and sugars together in a bowl until light and fluffy, then stir in the egg. Beat in the flour, baking powder and vanilla extract, then stir in three-quarters of the chocolate chips.

2 Use a teaspoon to dollop 24 walnut-sized balls of dough, well spaced apart, on to the prepared baking sheet and flatten gently. Scatter with the remaining chocolate chips and cook in the preheated oven, 190°C (375°F), Gas Mark 5, for 8-10 minutes until golden and just cooked through.

3 Leave the cookies to cool on a wire rack, then serve 2 cookies to each person, sandwiched together with a scoop of vanilla ice cream.

AFFORDABILITY
2

TIRAMISU

200 ml (7 fl oz) double cream
50 ml (2 fl oz) Marsala wine
250 g (8 oz) mascarpone
  cheese
4 tablespoons icing sugar
1 teaspoon vanilla extract
300 ml (½ pint) very strong
  coffee, cooled
20 sponge fingers
25 g (1 oz) plain dark chocolate,
  grated, to decorate

Serves **4**
Prep time **15 minutes, plus
  chilling**

1 Whisk the cream in a bowl until stiff peaks form. Reserve 1 tablespoon of the Marsala, then stir the remaining Marsala into the cream with the mascarpone, 3 tablespoons of the icing sugar and the vanilla extract.

2 Stir the remaining Marsala and icing sugar into the coffee, then dip 4 of the sponge fingers into the mixture and place each in the bottom of a glass or small serving dish. The sponge fingers should be just soft, not soggy.

3 Spoon some of the creamy mixture on top, then repeat the layers to use up the remaining ingredients. Chill in the refrigerator for 20 minutes, then serve sprinkled with grated chocolate.

AFFORDABILITY
3

STUDENT TIP

Student freezers are often filled with more ice than food. Don't wait until you can't shut the door: a regular defrost will help the freezer run more economically and maximize the storage space. This is a great revision-avoidance job.

SUMMER FRUIT GRATIN

1   Arrange all the fruit in a shallow ovenproof dish. Mix the mascarpone in a bowl with 2 tablespoons of the sugar, the cream and lime zest, then spoon over the fruit and spread into an even layer. Sprinkle the top with the remaining sugar.

2   Place the ovenproof dish on a baking sheet and bake in a preheated oven, 190°C (375°F), Gas Mark 5, for 15 minutes, or until the cheese has softened and the sugar topping has caramelized. Serve immediately.

VARIATION
For a tropical fruit gratin, arrange slices of 1 large mango in the dish with 1 sliced papaya and 150 g (5 oz) blueberries. Top with the mascarpone mix and bake as above.

2 peaches, halved, stoned and sliced
4 red plums, halved, stoned and sliced
150 g (5 oz) mixed raspberries and blackberries (or all raspberries)
200 g (7 oz) mascarpone cheese
4 tablespoons caster sugar
2 tablespoons double cream
grated zest of 1 lime

Serves **4**
Prep time **10 minutes**
Cooking time **20 minutes**

MANGO CRUMBLE
CHEESECAKE

1 Using a wooden spoon, beat the cream cheese in a bowl with the sugar and vanilla extract until softened. Add the eggs to one side of the bowl and tilt the bowl so you can beat the eggs to break them up thoroughly before combining them with the cream cheese. Beat in 1 teaspoon of the lime juice.

2 Turn into a shallow ovenproof dish – a small pie dish is ideal. Stand the dish in a roasting tin and pour a 2 cm (¾ inch) depth of boiling water from the kettle into the roasting tin. (Using the roasting tin and boiling water isn't essential but it helps bake the cheesecake evenly and stops it drying out around the edges.) Bake in a preheated oven, 160°C (325°F), Gas Mark 3, for 25-30 minutes until the cheesecake is lightly set around the edges but is still very wobbly in the centre.

3 While cooking, halve the mangoes either side of the flat stone. Cut away the skin and dice the flesh. Scatter the mango over the cheesecake and drizzle with the remaining lime juice. Crumble the cookies on top and sprinkle with the flaked almonds.

4 Return to the oven, in the roasting tin, for a further 10 minutes until the topping is lightly cooked. Serve warm, dusted with icing sugar, if liked.

500 g (1 lb) full-fat cream cheese
75 g (3 oz) caster sugar
1½ teaspoons vanilla extract
2 eggs
1 tablespoon lime juice
1 large or 2 small ripe mangoes
75 g (3 oz) crumbly oat or ginger cookies
3 tablespoons toasted flaked almonds
icing sugar, for dusting (optional)

Serves **4-5**
Prep time **10 minutes**
Cooking time **35-40 minutes**

Hot Caribbean
FRUIT SALAD

50 g (2 oz) unsalted butter
50 g (2 oz) light muscovado
sugar
1 large papaya, halved,
deseeded, peeled and sliced
1 large mango, peeled, stoned
and sliced
½ pineapple, skinned, cored
and cut into chunks
400 ml (14 fl oz) can coconut
milk
grated zest and juice of 1 lime

Serves **4**
Prep time **15 minutes**
Cooking time **10 minutes**

1 Melt the butter in a large frying pan, add the sugar and heat gently until just dissolved. Add all the fruit and cook for 2 minutes, then pour in the coconut milk and lime juice and add half the lime zest. Heat gently for 4-5 minutes, then serve warm in shallow serving bowls, sprinkled with the remaining lime zest.

3 tablespoons strong, freshly
   ground coffee (South Indian,
   Colombian or Javan)
1 teaspoon crushed cardamom
   seeds
250 ml (8 fl oz) milk
2 tablespoons sugar
600 ml (1 pint) water

Serves **4**
Prep time **5 minutes**
Cooking time **5 minutes**

CARDAMOM COFFEE

1 Place the coffee, cardamom seeds, milk, sugar and measured water in a large saucepan and bring to the boil. Reduce the heat and simmer for 1–2 minutes.

2 Using a very fine-meshed sieve lined with muslin, strain the coffee into mugs and serve hot.

3–4 lemon grass stalks, finely
   chopped
4 teaspoons Indian tea leaves
   (Darjeeling or Assam)
750 ml (1¼ pints) water

To serve
milk
sugar

Serves **4**
Prep time **5 minutes**
Cooking time **5 minutes**

LEMONGRASS TEA

1 Put the lemon grass and tea leaves in a large saucepan with the measured water and bring to the boil. Reduce the heat and simmer, uncovered, for 2–3 minutes.

2 Using a very fine-meshed sieve lined with muslin, strain the tea into mugs and serve hot, adding milk and sugar to taste.

Hot spiced ALMOND MILK

300 ml (½ pint) unsweetened
   almond milk or other nut milk
½ cinnamon stick
2 cloves
½ teaspoon vanilla extract
maple syrup, honey or soft brown
   sugar, to taste

To serve (optional)
ice cubes
freshly grated nutmeg

Serves **1**
Prep time **5 minutes, plus infusing**
Cooking time **5 minutes**

1 Pour the milk into a small saucepan, add the cinnamon and cloves and heat gently to almost boiling point, then turn off the heat and leave to infuse for at least 15 minutes, or overnight in the refrigerator.

2 Remove and discard the spices, then stir in the vanilla extract and maple syrup, honey or sugar to taste. Reheat if serving warm, or serve cold or chilled over ice. Sprinkle over a little nutmeg, if liked.

TROPICAL FRUIT *Smoothie*

1 Place all the ingredients in a food processor or blender and blitz until smooth. Pour into 4 glasses and serve immediately.

1 mango, peeled, stoned and chopped
2 kiwifruits, peeled and chopped
1 banana, cut into chunks
425 g (14 oz) can pineapple chunks or pieces in natural juice
450 ml (¾ pint) orange or apple juice
handful of ice cubes

Serves **4**
Prep time **10 minutes**

AFFORDABILITY 2

YOGURT & BERRY *Smoothie*

1 Place all the ingredients in a food processor or a blender and blitz until smooth. Pour into 4 glasses, decorate with a few extra whole berries and serve immediately.

300 ml (½ pint) natural yogurt
500 g (1 lb) fresh or frozen mixed summer berries, defrosted if frozen, plus extra to decorate
4 tablespoons millet flakes
3 tablespoons clear honey
300 ml (½ pint) cranberry juice

Serves **4**
Prep time **5 minutes**

INDEX

Acknowledgements

123RF.com 5second 165; akulamatiau 20; Baloncici 21a; foodandmore 183; hamik 21c; Hiromichi Koike 164; Joshua Resnick 21b, 148; Maxim Shebeko 182; oeytoja 82; Olena Danileiko 83; PaylessImages 205r; yelenayemchuk 164; Yulia Davidovich 205l

Octopus Publishing Group 65al, 109; David Munns 169al, 171; Emma Neish 28, 110, 166; Ian Garlick 122, 158; Ian Wallace 41, 51, 60, 65b, 84, 85, 97, 98, 107; Lis Parsons 10, 14, 26, 38, 48, 55, 57, 69, 73, 74, 90, 123b, 127, 130, 145; Stephen Conroy 2bl, 9b, 16, 22, 52, 65ar, 66, 70, 81, 83a & c, 87, 91, 92, 102, 123ar, 133, 134, 136, 137, 150, 162, 168, 169br, 173, 175, 187; Will Heap 27, 39, 40, 43, 44, 45, 89, 95, 101, 106, 111, 114, 115, 117, 118, 119, 121, 129, 159, 189al, 215, 217; William Reavell 146, 151, 152; William Shaw 2 a & br, 9al & ar, 11, 12, 15, 17, 19, 24, 25, 29, 31, 32, 33, 35, 36, 47, 49, 53, 56, 58, 59, 61, 62, 63, 64, 67, 71, 72, 75, 77, 78, 80, 94, 96, 99, 103, 104, 105, 112, 113, 123al, 125, 126, 128, 131, 135, 139, 141, 142, 143, 144, 155, 169 ar & bl, 176, 179, 181, 189 ar, bl & br, 190, 194, 197, 198, 199, 200, 201, 203, 207, 209, 210, 213, 214, 219a & b.

Publisher Sarah Ford
Extra recipes by Joanna Farrow
Features writer Cara Frost-Sharratt
Editor Natalie Bradley
Copy-editor Clare Churly
Proofreader Jane Birch
Indexer Isobel McLean
Senior Designer Jaz Bahra
Designer Jeremy Tilston
Production Controller Meskerem Berhane